A SHORT INTRODUCTION TO
CLINICAL
PSYCHOLOGY

Short Introductions to the Therapy Professions
Series Editor: Colin Feltham

Books in this series examine the different professions which provide help for people experiencing emotional or psychological problems. Written by leading practitioners and trainers in each field, the books are a source of up-to-date information about

- the nature of the work
- training, continuing professional development and career pathways
- the structure and development of the profession
- client populations and consumer views
- research and debates surrounding the profession.

Short Introductions to the Therapy Professions are ideal for anyone thinking about a career in one of the therapy professions or in the early stages of training. The books will also be of interest to mental health professionals needing to understand allied professions and also to patients, clients and relatives of service users.

Books in the series:

A Short Introduction to Clinical Psychology
Katherine Cheshire and David Pilgrim

A Short Introduction to Psychoanalysis
Jane Milton, Caroline Polmear and Julia Fabricius

A Short Introduction to Psychiatry
Linda Gask

A SHORT INTRODUCTION TO THE THERAPY PROFESSIONS

A SHORT INTRODUCTION TO
CLINICAL
PSYCHOLOGY

Katherine Cheshire and David Pilgrim

SAGE Publications
London • Thousand Oaks • New Delhi

First published 2004

SAGE Publications Ltd
1 Oliver's Yard
55 City Road
London EC1Y 1SP

SAGE Publications Inc.
2455 Teller Road
Thousand Oaks, California 91320

SAGE Publications India Pvt Ltd
B-42, Panchsheel Enclave
Post Box 4109
New Delhi 100 017

British Library Cataloguing in Publication data

A catalogue record for this book is available
from the British Library

ISBN 0 7619 4768 X
ISBN 0 7619 4769 8 (pbk)

Library of Congress Control Number: 2003115330

Typeset by C&M Digitals (P) Ltd., Chennai, India
Printed in Great Britain by TJ International Ltd, Padstow, Cornwall

CONTENTS

Preface   vi

Acknowledgements   viii

1   The Social and Historical Context of the Profession   1

2   The Knowledge Base of Clinical Psychology   24

3   Clinical Psychology Training   42

4   Careers in Clinical Psychology   64

5   Changing Practice and Changing Roles   85

6   Experts and Expertise   103

7   Internal and External Relationships   119

Glossary of Therapeutic Approaches   136

Further Reading   143

Appendix   144

References   145

Index   156

PREFACE

This book aims to provide an account of British clinical psychology that is both descriptive and critical. We have sought to give the reader an understanding of the profession's history, nature and function, while avoiding the self-serving public relations view that characterises much professional rhetoric. In order to facilitate our examination of these issues, we adopt a sociological framework that allows us to locate clinical psychology within the network that post-structuralists refer to as the psy complex: psychiatry, psychiatric social work, mental health nursing, counselling, psychotherapy and psychology. We argue that the contested knowledge base of British clinical psychology and its history (particularly its evolution within the National Health Service) are responsible for many of the profession's distinguishing features. At the same time, clinical psychology shares a number of characteristics with other members of the psy complex.

In the first two chapters of the book we provide the background to our subsequent exploration of contemporary British clinical psychology. In Chapter 1 we examine the social and historical context from which the profession emerged. Chapter 2 focuses on the knowledge base of the profession: its relationship with the academic discipline of psychology and its reliance on the scientist-practitioner model.

Chapters 3, 4 and 5 describe how prospective members gain entry to the profession and give an account of the work that we do, followed by a discussion of likely developments in our role. Chapter 3 begins with a view of clinical psychology training from the trainees' perspective, followed by an outline of current training arrangements and recent proposals to expand training provisions in order to meet the growing demand for our services. Chapter 4 contains a collection of accounts written by us and some of our colleagues, describing the current role of clinical psychologists with a range of client groups. In Chapter 5 we look more broadly at some of the emerging trends in clinical psychology and suggest some of the ways in which our role might evolve in the near future.

The last third of the book, Chapters 6 and 7, continues the critical appraisal of the profession that we began in Chapter 1. Chapter 6 extends the discussion of professional expertise, begun in Chapter 2, and examines how clinical psychology's credibility and marketability have developed on the basis of its claim to specific expertise within the psy complex. Finally, in Chapter 7, we assess both the internal and external relationships that define our profession. We start by discussing the divisions and co-dependencies within the profession, and then examine how clinical psychology continues to negotiate its boundaries with the NHS, central government, other professionals and service users. The book concludes with a brief consideration of some continuing debates in British clinical psychology that we expect to shape the attitudes and work of its members as we progress through its sixth decade. We suggest that the most radical shift in orientation may come from the growing influence of the Positive Psychology movement that champions the active promotion of psychological well-being in contrast with the exclusive focus on pathology, disorder and distress, which has traditionally characterised our work. If this shift occurs it may, at least in the short term, increase the gap between clinical psychology and other professions in the psy complex.

We hope that our readers find this book both informative and stimulating. Clinical psychology is still a very young profession but it is no longer in its infancy and we offer this contribution to debates about its nature and function in the belief that critical self-awareness is a sign of maturity within both individuals and organisations.

ACKNOWLEDGEMENTS

We would like to thank colleagues from the Fife Area Clinical Psychology Department, Stratheden Hospital, Cupar, Fife for their contributions to the following sections of Chapter 4:

Dr Steven Hughes: *Children and young people*
Dr Frances Baty: *Older adults*
Mr Bob Walley: *People with intellectual disabilities*
Ms Kate McGarva: *Clinical psychology in physical health care*
Mr Andy Peters: *Adults with substance misuse problems*
Dr Alan Harper: *Clinical neuropsychology*

1

THE SOCIAL AND HISTORICAL CONTEXT OF THE PROFESSION

Like all professions, clinical psychology has both features that it shares with other professions and characteristics that are peculiar to itself. In this introductory chapter we will first examine the nature of professions, drawing heavily on their sociology. This summary of sociological approaches to professional life should assist the reader to understand how clinical psychology reflects and reproduces general features of what came to be known during the twentieth century as the 'new middle class' (Carchedi, 1977). After this general sociological introduction we will identify one aspect of the particular character of British clinical psychology: its *history*. This history reflects the contested *knowledge base* of the profession – a subject we will return to in Chapter 2. In Chapter 6 we revisit this discussion by examining the ways in which this knowledge is expressed in British clinical psychology, both organisationally and rhetorically, as a form of *clinical expertise*. Our final chapter incorporates further discussion of the profession's internal dynamics and socio-political context and suggests how these factors are shaping its future.

What are professions?

The reader of this book, and of others in the series, can appraise the socio-political character of particular professions on a continuum from hostile scepticism to naïve trust. The former can be summarised in George Bernard Shaw's suggestion that 'the professions are a conspiracy against the laity'. This expression of outright distrust of self-serving professionals is also found in the sociology of the professions, as is its opposite: the view that professions are benign, altruistic and productive contributors to modern societies. In order to make sense of this range of views, and their potential applicability to clinical psychology, we will provide a summary of some sociological work about the mental health professions.

The mental health focus may seem overly restrictive, given that today clinical psychologists work in a variety of settings. However, the roots of the profession lie mainly in mental health work. Furthermore, in other clinical settings such as learning disability, child and adolescent services and physical health care, the profession finds itself, competitively or co-operatively, working alongside psychiatrists and other mental health professionals. Finally, the activities clinical psychologists are involved with in all health service contexts aim to improve well-being and quality of life, ameliorate distress, and reduce or control dysfunction. Taken together, these aims constitute mental health work in a very broad sense.

Clinical psychology is part of what poststructuralist sociologists call 'the psy complex' (Rose, 1985). Here the word 'complex' refers to a complex of professions (psychiatry, psychiatric social work, mental health nursing, counselling and psychotherapy) in interaction, with a variety of overlapping practices. The boundaries within this complex are murky, as we will show. Consequently, many of the issues considered in this text, although primarily focused on clinical psychology, necessarily address the psy complex in its totality.

Sociological accounts of modern professions

We noted above that views of the general public and of sociologists studying professions form a continuum. Saks (1983) compared sociological accounts of modern professions and identified three main types. The first, derived from the work of Emile Durkheim and Talcott Parsons, emphasised the functions of professions for society and the positive traits expected of, and delivered by, professionals (altruism, integrity, efficiency, unique skills, trustworthiness). This conservative trait and function approach no longer finds much favour within sociology, although professionals themselves may offer such descriptions as part of an exercise in collective self-promotion. Another point about this approach is that the very word 'professional' has entered the vernacular. It has come to mean efficient and trustworthy expertise. While sociologists have developed critical perspectives on the professions, our everyday discourse about them may still imply positive personal and social features.

The second approach to the professions suggested by Saks (1983) is derived from the work of Max Weber and remains the one most critical of the professions (more so than a Marxian approach: see p. 3 below). The neo-Weberian analysis of professions suggests that they act to exclude competitors in the market place and subordinate or dominate both their target client group and less-developed professions working in their field. Two notions in particular capture these processes: social closure and professional dominance.

Social closure entails professional groups advancing their interests in society by controlling their recruitment and excluding competitors. By these means they justify the maintenance and extension of both their economic value (fee or salary) and their social status and influence, by successfully convincing their employers and clientele that they possess unique expertise. This activity of closure entails professions regulating their own boundaries. Thus, entrance to a profession requires the acquisition of credentials and successful employment in a particular role. Those without this accredited and employed status are denied access to both privileged knowledge and forms of legitimate action, whether they are other workers or the profession's clients.

Professional dominance means that professionals try to acquire and maintain a dominant position in relation to others in society. This takes three forms. First, professionals have power over their clients, who are less knowledgeable and therefore may depend on professional expertise. Second, they have power over aspiring colleagues – applicants for training and those recently qualified. Third, they may acquire power over other professionals who have weaker claims to legitimacy because, for example, these latter professionals' knowledge base is less exclusive, their training is shorter or they lack formal legal powers (such as the power to detain a patient under the Mental Health Act). In particular, dominant professions will resist encroachment from other groups, whilst the latter will endeavour to encroach on work dominated by older professions or make bids for the legitimacy of new work.

A third sociological approach to the professions is that of the Marxian tradition. This approach has generated contradictory interpretations. Marxists can be found arguing that the professions constitute a part of the ruling class (Navarro, 1986); that they are part of the working class (the 'proletarianization' thesis: Oppenheimer, 1975); or that they constitute a new class in between the proletariat and the bourgeoisie. This last view of professionals, as a contradictory social group, has been argued by Carchedi (1977) and Johnson (1979). In their view the professions serve the interest of capital by forming a regulatory apparatus to maintain social stability in a capitalist society. However, when they are state employees (for example, in health and education) they are subject to bureaucratic subordination, which erodes their social power, making them wage slaves like any other worker.

Since Saks offered his overview of the sociology of the professions in the early 1980s, sociology has been influenced significantly by poststructuralism – especially the work of Michel Foucault. A fourth sociological position has emerged, arguing that power is dispersed and is not possessed clearly by one social group in relation to another (as suggested in different ways by Marx and Weber). Instead, the poststructuralists argue that power takes the form of discursive practices or discourses, which are precarious and can be challenged. At the same time, in their orthodox dominant forms, professionals and clients alike can share and be trapped in a particular set of practices and ways of framing reality. For example, professionals may have preferred ways of conceptualising and practising their work. Their current and potential clients can accept, ignore or resist this authority. Similarly, some in a profession may conform to an orthodox approach, while others may construct an alternative view.

A fifth current within recent sociological debates has been feminism, which at times has overlapped with Weberian, Marxian and poststructuralist accounts (Crompton, 1987; Pollert, 1996). The central organising concept is that of patriarchy, according to which some or all social divisions are accounted for by the political struggle between men and women, with the former dominating and the latter resisting. When this frame of analysis is applied to professional life a number of topics recur, including barriers to female entrants; obstacles to career advancement for women within professions; gendered divisions of labour within and between professional groups; the lower status and earning power of female-majority professions; and the experience of women as workers and mothers (Davies, 1996). Davies argues that the central issue for women is not their exclusion from the professions but the gendered way in which they are *included*. Another topic that has emerged within feminist debates about the professions is the gendered nature of professional knowledge, a point we return to in Chapter 6.

The applicability of sociologies of the professions to mental health work

We now turn to the relevance or 'fit' of different sociological approaches to the professions when mental health work is studied. We will focus on clinical psychology but allude at times to other professions. To focus on clinical psychology alone might mislead the reader by giving the impression that only this profession needs to be analysed critically; and the activity of clinical psychologists, like that of other professionals, occurs in an inter-professional context, especially in health care bureaucracies. Clinical psychology cannot be understood in isolation. We mentioned that the trait and function approach has fallen from favour within sociology. This approach, elaborated by Parsons, embraced the preferred accounts offered by professionals (especially professional leaders) and contemporary examples can be found in standard introductory texts about clinical psychology. One such 'public relations' view is provided in a recent account of the profession by two of its senior members:

> In summary, clinical psychologists are *psychologist-practitioners* applying *scientific knowledge and principles* in a *professional role* to the *alleviation of human suffering* and the *improvement of the quality of life.*
>
> (Marzillier and Hall, 1999: 9; italics in the original)

This view is the bread and butter of professional leaders' negotiations with employers and politicians. For example, when the Division of Clinical Psychology or the Professional Affairs Board of the BPS is asked to the negotiating table with civil servants, or its written comments on legislative or organisational change in the NHS are requested, it will take the opportunity to promote the interests of psychologists by stressing their special skills.

This activity is predicted most emphatically by the neo-Weberian approach to the professions, which suggests that they are perennially in the business of boundary maintenance, the making of new bids for legitimacy and the exploitation of opportunities for social advancement. Shaw was probably wrong to suggest that this happens conspiratorially *between* the professions, because they are frequently in competition with one another. For example, the activities of mental health nurses and of psychiatric social workers overlap. This creates the risk of one group substituting for the other (Rogers and Pilgrim, 2001). Clinical psychologists face a similar risk when they retain a therapist-only role in their work since those trained in psychological therapies from other professions, such as mental health nursing, can also fill that role. In order to counteract this threat, leaders of the profession have argued that psychologists employ unique skills within the therapist role (Parry, 1989; Hallam et al., 1989). In the 1980s, when the role of psychologists in the NHS was examined by government, boundary maintenance was negotiated successfully by leaders arguing that clinical psychologists alone have 'level 3' therapy skills (see, p. 18 below).

Clinical psychology is one of the highest-salaried non-medical professions and yet it is predominantly a female profession.

Concerns about women undermining the social status and salary levels of clinical psychology have been publicly expressed by some men (Crawford, 1989; Radford and Holdstock, 1995). The point made by Davies about the peculiar ways in which women are included in the profession is relevant here. Although the majority of the profession is female, men are over-represented in senior management roles (Murray and McKenzie, 1998).

As we noted in the introduction to this chapter, generalisations in the sociological literature on the professions beg particular questions about individual professions. In the present discussion this prompts us to acquaint the reader with relevant details from the history of British clinical psychology.

A short history of British clinical psychology

In the early days of British clinical psychology, one of its professional leaders, Hans Eysenck, noted that 'psychology has a long past, but a short history' (Eysenck, 1953: 22). In this book we will explore the meaning of this claim. Clinical psychology is one of several specialist applications based upon what is now the single academic discipline of psychology. However, while psychology is typically organised in dedicated university departments, its theoretical and empirical concerns overlap with those of its neighbours, such as philosophy, other human sciences (e.g. anthropology and sociology) and the biological sciences (e.g. physiology and neurology).To understand this connection to other academic disciplines, clinical psychology's 'prehistory', as well as its history, needs to be examined. In this chapter we will first deal with the period just prior to the profession's formation in the 1950s and then with its development after that time. Finally, some points will be made regarding North American influences on the development of clinical psychology in Britain.

Academic psychology becomes established in Britain

By the end of the nineteenth century it was becoming evident that the discipline of psychology was about to differentiate itself from philosophy. This first took place in Germany, with other countries such as Britain and the USA catching up within a few decades. The earlier developments in Germany meant that the German model of experimental work was influential for a while across both the Atlantic and the English Channel, with pioneers such as Weber, Fechner, Helmholtz, Lotze and Müller first defining the academic field.

In Britain, the work of Francis Galton (Darwin's cousin) and the social movement of eugenics ensured that an evolutionary perspective would become important in both British psychology and psychiatry. Its specific impact on later clinical work derived from the notion that innate individual differences between people could be measured – the beginnings of the psychometric measurement of intelligence and personality that became known as differential psychology. This hereditarian focus was at odds with the older empiricist tradition in Britain, and subsequent developments (for example in Eysenck's methodological behaviourism) reflected a principled acceptance of the variable interaction between genes and learning. Methodological considerations in this nascent period emphasised experimentalism, psychometrics, the hypothetico-deductive method and the use of statistical methods to map populations and define experimental and control groups.

In the academy, the differentiation from philosophy was slow, with leaders of the parent discipline retarding the independence of psychology. By the outbreak of the Second World War, there were still only six chairs in psychology in the British academic system (Hearnshaw, 1964), despite the emergence of a dedicated professional organisation at the turn of the century. The Psychological Society was inaugurated at University College, London, in 1901, taking the term 'British' in 1906 to become what is still called the British Psychological Society (BPS). In 1902 its membership was a mere 13 and the BPS remained a tiny club of philosophers and psychologically minded medical practitioners until the First World War (Edgell, 1961).

Soon after the BPS was founded, the *British Journal of Psychology* was also set up (although this was, to begin with, separate from the Society). In the very first statement from the founding editors, James Ward and W.H.R. Rivers, the remit of the new discipline was announced:

> Psychology, which till recently was known among us chiefly as mental philosophy and was widely concerned with problems of a more or less speculative and transcendental character, has now at length achieved the position of a positive science; one of special interest to the philosopher no doubt, but still independent of his control, possessing its own methods, its own specific problems and a distinct standpoint altogether its own. 'Ideas' in the philosophical sense do not fall within its scope; its inquiries are restricted entirely to facts. (Editorial, *British Journal of Psychology*, 1904, 1 (1): 1)

Given the slow organisational separation of psychology from philosophy in the academy during the first quarter of the twentieth century, Ward and Rivers were being rhetorical rather than accurately descriptive. Indeed, they were setting out the stall for the new academic discipline and their emphasis upon the pursuit of 'facts', together with their insistence on psychology being a 'positive science', is therefore important. The central orthodoxy in British psychology was and still is positivistic, although philosophical idealism has been a constant thorn in its flesh (most recently this has been evident in the emergence of postmodernism within academic psychology). Psychology made its initial claim for separate legitimacy by emphasising objectivity and empiricism as the features that distinguished it from philosophy, which was preoccupied with metaphysics and logic. While philosophy was a cerebral activity, relying on speculation, introspection and reflection, psychologists had begun to test experimental hypotheses and devise practical interventions based on emerging theories.

Developments in the USA followed a similar pattern although the differentiation of psychology from philosophy occurred slightly earlier and was driven by members of both disciplines. For example, in their textbooks at the end of the nineteenth century both William James and John Dewey explored the need to shift from philosophy to psychology, while recognising the debt owed to the former by the latter (James, 1890; Dewey, 1886). It is significant that although Dewey was a philosopher, he championed pragmatism in his discipline. The special relationship between Britain and its ex-colony has led to an identifiable form of Anglo-American psychology over the past century, but British developments have generally tended to follow trends originating in the USA.

Popular and professional psychology in Britain 1900–50

Although the emancipation of psychology from philosophy, marked by the founding of the Psychological Society in 1901, was essential for its emergence as an independent discipline, Thomson (2001) argues that the subsequent development of British academic and professional psychology can only be fully understood by charting their evolving relationships with popular psychology during the first half of the twentieth century. In the following section we will summarise some of the main points contained in Thomson's informative account of this relationship.

While the organised discipline of psychology was still in its infancy, a vigorous self-help culture with its origins in nineteenth-century movements like phrenology was flourishing in Britain. Popular psychology then, as now, was pluralist and maintained a strained relationship with the medical profession. In the same year that the British Psychological Society was formed, the London Psycho-Therapeutic Society was established as an ecumenical forum to promote the 'psychic' interests of Spiritualists, Theosophists, the Mental Science, Christian Science and Divine Science Movements. The Society's members were not only committed to investigating psychic forces, but also wished to apply them therapeutically – hence the antagonism of the medical establishment. As the century unfolded, the Society increasingly sought to distance itself from the religious movements it had encompassed through its membership by reinterpreting psychic power as a manifestation of 'natural law': the health of the mind and body now became acknowledged goals, instead of spiritual health alone.

The psychotherapeutic emphasis of the Society was initially influenced by continental psychology's interest in hypnotism and suggestion, while psycho-magnetics and mesmerism also featured in the treatments offered by its members. However, influential popular writers like Emile Coué, C. Harry Brooks and Dr Bernard Hollander, Britain's leading phrenologist and a frequent contributor to the *Psycho-Therapeutic Journal/Health Record*, subsequently led the trend away from reliance on experts to cure society's ills. Instead, these authors encouraged people to harness their own healing power through healthy living, self-control and auto-suggestion. Coué, for example, exhorted the use of positive affirmations to promote mental health in his widely read self-help manual: *Self Mastery through Conscious Autosuggestion* (1922).

By the 1920s this interest in self-help had produced a new front in the lay psychology movement and its members identified themselves as practical psychologists. The Federation of Practical Psychology Clubs of Great Britain emerged, with its own journal: *Practical Psychologist*. By the end of the 1930s there were over 50 clubs throughout England and Scotland, coexisting with smaller lay psychology movements and unaffiliated individuals pursuing their own psychological studies and enquiries. Thomson suggests that the vigour of these popular movements is understandable because they met a number of societal needs, including a demand for psychological therapy that the medical professionals were unable to deal with.

One of the important features of Practical Psychology was that it professed to be scientific in its approach to self-improvement. Its founder, Anna Maud Hallam, described its approach in the inaugural edition of *Practical Psychologist*:

PRACTICAL psychology is a scientific effort to unfold and understand the laws operating in human life....This great study of human life brings new enlightenment, new education, new and clearer understanding of the phenomena of every-day life. It is an effort based upon unbiased investigation, research, experiment and observation, with just one motive underlying it – to assist the individual in knowing himself. (Hallam, 1925: 1)

Thus, the Practical Psychologists set out their stall by claiming intellectual rigour and scientific credibility. The distinction they drew between their own work and that of the academic psychologists was merely one of orientation:

Academic psychology will centre the cause of these mental conflicts in the various human instincts. The student of practical psychology will explain them under the caption of the subconscious mind where all instincts, emotions and inclinations have their origin. (Hallam, 1925: 2)

While asserting its scientific credentials, Practical Psychology retained a spiritual dimension. Its goal was personal enlightenment, and it couched this in language that appealed to both humanists and committed Christians. The movement thus ensured itself a substantial following.

From its initially competitive position in relation to academic psychology, Practical Psychology adopted a less combative stance during successive years. As medically qualified psychotherapists joined the fray, Practical Psychology increasingly assumed the role of 'populist intermediary' (Thomson, 2001) between the professionals and the public. By the end of the 1930s, Practical Psychologists had begun to write self-help manuals focusing on problems identified by academics and professional psychologists (such as inferiority complexes and nervous tension), instead of guides to self-enlightenment.

As Thomson points out, the influence between professional and lay psychology was not unidirectional. The popularisation of psychology appeared immensely threatening to professional psychologists who were insecure about the scientific foundations of their young discipline, and they initially fought back by attacking the unscientific nature of the popular treatises. However, as the century progressed, some members of the profession began to recognise the potential of popular psychology to extend the influence of the discipline and some of them, like Cyril Burt, began to write (and even broadcast) with a wider audience than the academic community in mind. The boundary work of these psychologists involved educating the public about matters psychological in a way that would convince them that psychology was scientific and sufficiently complex to merit the employment of experts as disseminators of this knowledge. The British mental hygiene movement represents a more co-ordinated attempt by the professionals to popularise psychological theory in order to advise the public on how to lead a psychologically healthy life. Thomson suggests that this movement's limited success was at least partly due to the profession's ambivalence about the extent to which they were prepared to give psychology away.

Thomson's account of the relationship between professional psychologists and these popular movements in the first half of the twentieth century is relevant to our discussion for several reasons. First, it provides a counterbalance to the poststructuralist view of psychology during this period as a conservative if not oppressive force dedicated to social adjustment. Second, it demonstrates the falsity of the view that popular psychology is a recent product of professional psychology, and essentially a watered-down version of the latter. Instead, it describes the origins of what we now term the users' movement and shows that the profession has had to engage in boundary work throughout its existence – not only with other professions (psychiatry, in particular) and other disciplines (such as medicine and science), but also with the general public. Finally, Thomson argues that the popular psychology movement arose to meet a demand that was not being met by academic psychologists or the medically qualified therapists of the period.

Jones and Elcock (2001) have suggested that 'disciplinary psychology' is still failing to meet the public demand for what they term 'everyday psychology': the psychologising we all do, all the time, in order to make sense of our world. They conclude that 'scientific psychology' needs to make renewed efforts to be relevant to this, to be accessible while retaining theoretical and evidential rigour, in order to contribute to a shared, informed view of the world. We will consider these issues in greater detail in the next chapter.

The emergence of clinical psychology in Britain

The major historical roots of British clinical psychology can be traced to events surrounding the First and Second World Wars. Dominant forms of psychology that had emerged from the academy (psychoanalysis, differential psychology and learning theory) were challenged and influenced in the context of war and post-war conditions between 1914 and 1950. After 1914 the problem of shell-shock, or war neurosis, was an important spur for developing psychological formulations and treatments (Stone, 1985). The men breaking down in the trenches were 'England's finest blood' and not the 'tainted gene pool' which, it was commonly assumed, had inhabited the asylums and workhouses. The soldier-patients were both officers and gentlemen and squaddie volunteers, with the first group actually breaking down at a higher rate than the second (Salmon, 1917). In this context, the eugenic bio-determinism favoured by asylum doctors was seen as a sort of treason. Consequently, it fell from favour in government circles, creating a political space for the growth of psychological approaches.

In 1919 the first section of the BPS to be formed was the Medical (now Psychotherapy) Section and it was dominated by doctors returning from their war work, treating victims of shell-shock. In the same year the British Psycho-Analytical Society was established, with an overlapping membership. During the war, increasing interest had been taken in psychosomatic aspects of fatigue, with the focus particularly on the overworked female employees in the munitions factories. The Health of Munitions Workers Committee (later renamed the Industrial Fatigue Board) was set up by Lloyd George in 1915 and was subsumed by the Medical Research Council in 1929. This formed the focus for the early development of industrial psychology in Britain, with Cyril Burt and others beginning to apply psychological methods within the military-industrial complex.

Thus, it was the costly state-endorsed violence of the 'Great War' that was the biggest political spur to the development of applied psychology. The doctors returning from military service contributed to the status and influence of what was to become one of two key training bases for clinical psychology: the Tavistock Clinic. During the 1930s, with another war becoming inevitable, the Ministry of Defence recruited psychologists and psychotherapists to oversee selection procedures in an attempt to filter out emotionally vulnerable military applicants. An indication of the status of the psychoanalytic tradition in this period was that the appointed head of the army psychiatric services in 1939, J.R. Rees, was a psychoanalyst. He had been director of the Tavistock Clinic since 1934.

During the Second World War the role of psychologists and psychotherapists within the military expanded yet further. In addition to recruitment and selection, they were increasingly involved in training, and in the prevention and detection of malingering (Bourke, 2001). The demand for psychological treatment also increased substantially as the new hostilities with Germany saw the return of war neurosis. (During this conflict, 20–50 per cent of all military discharges were the result of psychological trauma: Bourke, 2001.) A variety of hospital settings were utilised to treat what has now become known as 'post-traumatic stress disorder'. In 1942 Hans Eysenck was appointed as a research psychologist at one of these bases: the Mill Hill Emergency Hospital.

When Mill Hill was reconstituted at Camberwell after the war, it formed the basis of the new Institute of Psychiatry with several academic departments that were linked to clinical services in the Maudsley Hospital. Eysenck was appointed as head of psychology at the Institute. The first clinical psychology course, based at the Institute, was limited to the psychometric assessment of patients and emphasised the role of psychologist, not as therapist, but as *applied researcher*. This tension between the healing role with its fluid intersubjective character on one side, and the 'disinterested scientific stance' of the psychological researcher on the other (Eysenck, 1949, 1950), continues to characterise the profession to this day.

The development of British clinical psychology after 1950

Postgraduate clinical psychology training initially developed at three sites in Great Britain – the Tavistock Clinic and the Institute of Psychiatry in London, and the Crichton Royal Hospital in Dumfries, Scotland. In 1957 these became the first three courses to be recognised within the government's Whitley Council negotiating system for the NHS. While the Tavistock tradition, based upon psychoanalysis, was to drive the therapeutic community movement post-war, Eysenck's course would become the dominant influence in the profession. For many years to come, new courses set up throughout Britain (usually, but not always, in the old universities with medical schools) were headed up by Institute/Maudsley graduates.[1] Between 1950 and 1980 the profession developed through three phases (psychometrics, behaviour therapy and eclecticism) that reflected epistemological and professional tensions (Pilgrim and Treacher, 1992).

The *psychometric* phase of British psychology was short-lived (1950–58). At first Hans Eysenck insisted that experimentalism and the psychology of individual differences (in the tradition of University College, London dating back, via Burt and Spearman, to Galton and his eugenic acolytes in the late Victorian period) should characterise the work of clinical psychologists. Intelligence testing and personality assessments looked set to define the new profession in quite narrow terms. Indeed, when Eysenck visited the USA in 1948 to look at clinical psychology programmes, he took his American colleagues to task, arguing that their therapeutic aspirations were at odds with the disinterested stance required by a scientific attitude (Eysenck, 1949, 1950). Eysenck saw therapy as 'essentially alien to clinical psychology' (Eysenck, 1949: 173), a view that survived in the profession long after Eysenck recanted his position. At the Crichton Royal Hospital, Dumfries, for example, another psychometrician and professional leader, John Raven, continued to argue, during the 1960s, that therapy was outside the legitimate remit of clinical psychology (Hetherington, 1981).

In fact, arguments about whether psychometrics should partially or wholly define the role of clinical psychologists had started in the USA as early as 1913. There, the profession emerged more than thirty years before it did in Britain. By 1917, the short-lived American Association of Clinical Psychologists had been established, to be superseded two years later by the enduring structure of the Clinical Section of the American Psychological Association. By the time Eysenck did his rapid audit-by-visit after the Second World War psychometric assessment was still an important role for clinicians in the USA, but it had been joined by a range of psychotherapeutic activities as well – some based on psychoanalysis and others on behaviourism.

The psychometric phase of British clinical psychology gave way in the late 1950s to *behaviour therapy*, with Eysenck and his colleagues Monte Shapiro and Gwynne-Jones suddenly shifting their focus in a bid to wrest psychiatry's control of the therapeutic jurisdiction of neurosis. This bid was made very publicly in a paper Eysenck presented, with Gwynne-Jones, to the Royal Medico-Psychological Association (since 1971, the Royal College of Psychiatrists) and represented a notable ideological U-turn by Eysenck (Eysenck 1949, 1958). We will reconsider these events in more detail in Chapter 2 when we discuss the genesis of the scientist-practitioner model in British clinical psychology.

The third phase of the profession was one of *eclecticism*. This ensued because clinical psychology failed to develop a firm consensus about its core role. Although an official stance regarding the psychologist as scientist-practitioner had remained predominant in both the American Psychological Association and the BPS since the early 1950s (Raimy, 1953; Shapiro, 1951), it had failed wholly to displace other theoretical strands (particularly variants of phenomenology and psychoanalysis). By the 1970s, pluralism had become commonplace in NHS departments. This was reinforced by the shift in academic psychology from behaviourism to cognitivism, which was paralleled by a (theoretically contradictory) orthodoxy of cognitive-behavioural methods of treatment. Hybrids of cognitivism and depth psychology, such as cognitive-analytic therapy, also emerged. For the past twenty years clinical psychology has retained this eclectic and pluralistic character.

Self-regulation in British clinical psychology: the 1970s and beyond

Until the late 1970s there were few signs of clinical psychologists seeking to advance their status through formal state recognition. Although psychologists disagreed with one another about their role and its content, they all accepted that their academic credentials were sufficient to justify their social legitimacy and employment status. Whilst there had been no proactive interest from the Ministry (now Department) of Health in the post-war years in converting clinical psychology into a registered profession, during the 1970s a number of concerns began to emerge about 'mind-bending techniques'. In the early 1970s, the Church of Scientology had attempted to infiltrate and take over the largest British mental health charity, MIND. This crisis stimulated an official investigation (Foster, 1971) into the role and impact of scientology, which offers a form of psychotherapy called 'dianetics'.

Foster recommended that there should be state registration of psychotherapists but his prompt to government remained unheeded, although private psychoanalytic organisations (i.e. not the BPS) maintained a lobby to support some form of registration. Another report was then commissioned and in 1978 the Seighart Report on the registration of psychotherapists was published, supporting Foster (Seighart, 1978). Once again, these recommendations failed to stimulate government action over new legislation.

Meanwhile, the Trethowan Report on the role of psychologists in the NHS (DHSS, 1977) had given the green light for clinical psychology's formal separation from psychiatry. Since 1958, when clinical psychologists moved presumptuously into the medical territory of treatment, relationships between the two professions had deteriorated. By the mid-1970s clinical psychologists were increasingly resistant to efforts by psychiatric colleagues to maintain leadership in NHS mental health services. As GPs began to refer patients directly to clinical psychologists, the profession no longer had to depend on psychiatrists to provide it with work. Within localities relationships between psychologists and their psychiatric colleagues generally became more distant and, in some instances, openly confrontational.

The Trethowan Report was produced during the 1980s by a sub-committee of the DHSS Standing Mental Health Advisory Committee under the leadership of Professor W.H. Trethowan, and it represented the first major official statement about the organisation and management of clinical psychology services in the NHS. The Secretary of State broadly welcomed its recommendations, while commending to the various health authorities only those recommendations without financial implications. The BPS also welcomed the Report and it provided the model for organisation of clinical psychology services for the next twenty years – until the introduction of NHS Trusts under the Conservative government began to dismantle service structures that spanned more than one Trust.

The Trethowan Report recommended that services should be organised on an area basis and be provided by area departments of clinical psychology. It did not define what, specifically, it meant by 'Area Department', but the implication was that clinical psychologists would no longer be employed by specific hospitals or services, but would be accountable to the employing Health Authority through the Area Department. The report also proposed that these departments should contain a number of specialist sections, with a total of eight sections envisaged for a fully developed area department, namely: physical handicap; mental handicap; child health (child psychiatry and paediatrics); neurological science; mental illness (including forensic psychiatry and psychotherapy); geriatrics; adolescent services; and primary health care. Thus, departments would offer a generic service although individual clinicians would specialise in work with particular client groups. The BPS concluded that area departments had four main advantages: (1) they could allocate their resources as they saw fit to best meet the needs of the population served, rather than being constrained by the individual contractual ties of clinicians to particular hospitals/services; (2) they allowed for both exchange of ideas and enhanced professional support among clinicians, thus reducing professional isolation; (3) they promoted increased efficiency in clinical psychology training (by allowing trainees to move between specialist sections within the same department) and (4) they contributed to higher professional standards (McPherson, 1983). As noted above, the creation of area departments of clinical psychology also shifted the power balance between psychiatry and psychology in the modernising NHS.

The juxtaposition of the Seighart and Trethowan Reports marked a turning point, and increasing efforts at self-determination in the profession ensued. However, after 1979 these efforts were made in the face of growing hostility to professional autonomy on the part of the British government. Margaret Thatcher's project of (partial) re-commodification of the welfare state was to affect all public sector employees, including clinical psychologists.

In 1979 the Division of Clinical Psychology (DCP) rejected the Seighart recommendation on *psychotherapy* registration but immediately began work on developing a case for government for the registration of *clinical psychologists* in the UK. The plan to register psychotherapists brought with it the danger of state recognition of a motley group of therapists with their own forms of applied psychological knowledge. In order to ward off this competing bid for legitimacy from those outside the profession, the DCP pushed for registration on its own terms for its own practitioners.

By seeking to operationalise the mandate to practise as an applied psychologist, in terms that coincided with the pre-existing credentials of DCP members, the profession was pursuing a strategy that was doubly advantageous. It would exclude competitors who were not qualified in academic psychology and it would mean that the DCP did not have to define precisely what psychology *was* (except in the circular sense of it being what is taught at a particular time to undergraduates studying psychology). This was important, given the contested nature of psychological knowledge. While some professions like dentistry or surgery can operationalise their knowledge base with a degree of contemporary certainty, this is considerably more difficult in psychology.

Psychological knowledge has always been divided, with incommensurable epistemological strands at its heart (Foucault, 1973; Smart, 1990). Human experience and conduct are complex and thus open to many types of conceptualisation and forms of practical investigation. Phenomenology, experimentalism, differential psychology, behaviourism, psychoanalysis, cognitivism and, latterly, social constuctionism have jostled for position and ebbed and flowed in fashion, in undergraduate studies and postgraduate training. All have had their devotees, and factionalism has been guaranteed.

In this context it would be nigh impossible for the BPS, at any point in time, to offer to government for serious consideration a coherent *definition*, let alone a coherent body of knowledge, which summarised the agreed content of the academic discipline of psychology, or the scope of work of its professional wings (such as the DCP). Emergent qualities which psychology graduates may possess, as a result of the contested terrain of their discipline, are a tolerance of uncertainty and a tendency to examine knowledge claims sceptically. However, these laudable intellectual virtues have not been overly-emphasised by the profession, when it has pleaded to government for privileged recognition.

In the 1980s a phase of *managerialism* succeeded the earlier focus on irresolvable epistemological tensions within the profession (Pilgrim, 1990). The term 'managerialism' had a double significance during that time. Not only did the profession set out more formally to establish the conditions of self-management but it also had to adapt to a central government policy of imposed general management. The campaign for registration in the 1980s was driven initially by the DCP but very soon the wider leadership within the BPS took up the cause. Between 1984 and 1988 the sheer volume of work required to advance the cause of registration and adapt to the demands of general management in the NHS meant that the DCP had to appoint a full-time employee to manage this bureaucratic complexity.

The more mature profession of medicine reacted pugnaciously during this period to the pressures caused by the bureaucratic subordination being imposed by Thatcher's government. The smaller and less secure profession of clinical psychology proceeded more cautiously. Some psychologists (like many nurses) secured posts as general managers. The profession's leadership agreed to a review by the Manpower Advisory Group (MPAG) of the Department of Health. This was a controversial move, with a vociferous minority in the profession making a failed bid for a vote of no confidence in the leadership. The internal critics argued that, given Thatcher's hostility to the health professions, the time was not right to bare a collective throat.

The manpower review was relevant to the chances of professional advancement in an unpredictable way. Published in 1988, it had no catastrophic effect on the profession but gave little clear indication of how its positive recommendations might be applied within an NHS structure, which was being rapidly fragmented by quasi-marketisation. The main advantage of the review to the profession was not that it justified the employment of a certain number of psychologists in the NHS but it provided a focus for its identity. A leading clinical psychologist and member of the MPAG made the point that:

> The 1980s has been about establishing who we are, what we can do and what is our core identity. If you like it is has been about establishing a proper rhetoric of justification. The hostile climate for professionals has put pressure on us to clarify and justify what we are about. (Parry, 1990, cited in Pilgrim, 1990)

As it turned out, Derek Mowbray, the consultant employed by the MPAG to review the state of clinical psychology, created an opportunity for it to make a claim of uniqueness. He argued that the broad-based higher education in psychological knowledge that clinical psychologists enjoyed put them in a special position to offer skills to the NHS. Mowbray's argument was that psychological skills could be divided into three levels. Level 1 skills are used to establish rapport or conduct simple interventions like stress management. Level 2 skills are used in more complex interventions, but are reducible to manual-based techniques that can be followed like recipes. Level 3 skills, however, are required when therapists offer unique psychological formulations and interventions in particular person–situation contexts. Mowbray proffered the view that only clinical psychology could offer level 3 skills, with levels 1 and 2 being offered by other health workers.

Thus, by 1990, clinical psychology had an official report arguing for the profession's unique skills and it had secured the right to keep its own register of qualified practitioners. It had not managed to ensure mandatory registration of its membership, although the leadership of the profession has maintained a campaign for this to the present time, and it is now imminent (see Chapter 7). Meanwhile, the discourse about the registration of psychotherapists has also continued. After many years of internecine disputes and tentative alliances between therapists with a vast array of training backgrounds, the United Kingdom Council for Psychotherapy was set up in 1993. Since then the UKCP has pressed for the registration of its members. However, at the time of writing, there remains no legal requirement for psychotherapists to be registered.

During most of the 1990s the profession pursued new forms of legitimacy. In the early 1990s a three-year doctoral programme replaced the two-year master's programmes in clinical psychology as the required professional training. A form of mimicry of medicine had already begun in the 1980s, with some members of the most senior ('Top') grade in the profession adopting the new title of 'Consultant'. The adoption of the title of 'Dr' by all new entrants to clinical psychology completed the emulation of the profession that had previously subordinated the work of psychologists. As medical practitioners generally do not hold a doctorate, and so claim 'Dr' as an honorary prefix, psychologists, and latterly pharmacists, are now arguably 'out-doctoring' the medics. Today, the salary levels of clinical psychologists remain below those of medical practitioners, but not by much. In many ways clinical psychologists have accrued the very trappings of a profession that was previously a source of resented constraint. One observer has suggested that, during the 1970s, clinical psychologists began a campaign not only of escape from medical domination, but also of incremental emulation and reactive encroachment (Clare, 1979).

Discussion: the influence of the past on the present

This chapter has outlined sociological debates and has highlighted some key historical influences on the development of clinical psychology in Britain. Some general summary points can be made here:

- Our main concern in this book is to provide an account of clinical psychology from a British perspective. Empiricism has had a profound influence within our culture. Its historical power is evident internationally but its enduring native influence is also significant. For example, psychoanalysis was an interloper in British culture and, as a consequence, it has either been derided in British clinical psychology (a position championed by Hans Eysenck in the 1950s) or contained on the exotic margins of private practice and medical psychotherapy. By contrast, psychometrics, behaviour therapy and cognitive-behaviour therapy, with their roots in the work of Galton, Locke and Hartley, are British in character and so rest comfortably within our cultural orthodoxy. British clinical psychology is certainly pluralistic but there remains a core orthodoxy of psychometrics and elaborated methodological behaviourism – first behaviour therapy and now cognitive-behaviour therapy. This core orthodoxy largely defines the taught curriculum for British clinical psychology trainees.

- Despite the virtual separation of philosophy from medicine until the nineteenth century, psychiatry became an important force in shaping the character of clinical psychology. It seems that clinical psychology can neither live happily with psychiatry nor without it. Once *clinical* psychology was established as a profession (beyond being part of an academic discipline of psychology) it began to behave like other professions. It defined its boundaries and made bids for legitimacy to claim both expertise over its client group and differentiation from established professions. In a clinical context, the latter meant a struggle for autonomy from a medical speciality: psychiatry.

- The emergence of the profession has historical foundations beyond its relationship with the older dominant groups in the academy and clinic. In particular, wartime conditions and public policy structures (such as our health care system) were important. We have also noted the spur to the development of the profession that was provided by the vigorous popular psychology movement in Britain. To understand the profession in historical terms requires some understanding of these influences.

Some further reflections can be offered about our cultural legacy. The brief historic account above has missed out huge chunks of commentary about non-British influences on clinical psychology in an international context.

The content of clinical psychology's theory and practice is not uniform internationally. Whilst similarities exist across countries and continents, each has its own national and cultural motif. For example, our account in this book emphasises quite a narrow range of influences before 1900. Apart from some temporary modelling on German academic pioneers, British empiricist philosophy and Galtonian eugenics (with its cue for the psychology of individual differences) have determined our professional orthodoxy. When we look elsewhere, we find a slightly more variegated picture.

When John Reisman was faced with writing a history of clinical psychology from a US perspective in the mid-1960s (Reisman, 1966), he mentioned a wide range of influences before 1900. These certainly included the British empiricists, who provided the philosophical soil for North American behaviourism to take root and flourish, but he also highlights the French influence in the work of Rousseau and Pinel. Murphy (1928), a US historian of psychology in the early twentieth century, pointed to other French influences: in particular, the work of Condillac, Charcot and Mesmer. From a North American perspective, it might also be significant that Reisman emphasises the political unrest which characterised France, Germany, Russia and his own country during the nineteenth century. Dramatic historical events (for example the war of independence, 'conquering' the western frontier and the consequent genocide of native people, civil war, and the abolition of slavery) were mirrored in North American human science, which has built larger and bolder theoretical structures than its British equivalent.

The internal boundary-breaking of the USA and its imperialist adventures abroad became cultural features which shaped its native psychology. By contrast Britain, with its peculiar island mentality, was a declining colonial power at the start of the twentieth century. British psychology and its applied clinical wing to some degree reflect the mood of this historical period. They have been conservative, empiricist, pragmatic, and incrementalist and have tended to eschew a commitment to theoretical systems building (a task left to others abroad). A number of examples reinforce this point. Although British empiricism may have been the philosophical source of the type of cognitive therapy practised recently in British clinical psychology, its theoretical rationale is located in American work. Even when developments were fairly a-theoretical or eclectic, the seminal *rationales* for clinical work originated in the USA. Cognitive-behaviour therapy (CBT) and rational emotive behaviour therapy (REBT) were instigated by the American psychiatrists Aaron Beck and Albert Ellis respectively. Clinical leadership in CBT innovations continues to be dominated by American psychologists (such as Marsha Linehan and Christine Padesky). It is true that the main instigator of cognitive-analytic therapy (CAT) was a British general practitioner (Ryle, 1990). However, its theoretical roots were in American humanism (George Kelly's personal construct therapy), continental psychoanalysis and Russian neuropsychology.

While James Watson, B.F. Skinner and the American learning theorists developed the British empiricist principles (and indeed some of the physiological work of Hartley), as did Bechterev and Pavlov in pre-Revolutionary Russia, British clinical psychology has found itself reimporting philosophical premises shaped elsewhere. Even the modest theoretical positions that have been championed (for example the methodological behaviourism underpinning British behaviour therapy in the late 1950s and early 1960s) were associated with intellectual émigrés (Hans Eysenck, Jack Rachman, Monte Shapiro and Victor Meyer). A consequence of our post-colonial, empiricist and pragmatic culture has been a relative absence of home-grown theoretical innovation. Our 'special relationship' with the USA in disciplinary terms has ensured that the North American academic culture has had a continuous influence on British professional practice and concerns. This reflects an enduring, if selective, intellectual reliance upon the grander scale and content of North American psychology.

Thus, the development of clinical psychology in Britain over the past hundred years can be understood in relation to a number of dynamics and factors. The knowledge base inherited from the longer history Eysenck alludes to, cited above, is important. However, the specific culture of Britain is also relevant – both to the empiricism that influenced the emerging profession, and the structural constraints that moulded it within the National Health Service. As will be clear in the rest of the book, the context of the profession contains both epistemological and organisational features that need to be understood as a whole system.

This chapter has introduced a number of threads of understanding about British clinical psychology. As an interest group it needs to be understood sociologically. As a culture with a contested range of ideas and practices it needs to be understood historically. As a form of applied human science its peculiarities need to be explored because professions that deal with other human beings are special and, within that group, those claiming expertise in human behaviour and experience are particularly special. These themes about the socio-historical nature of the profession will be explored further in the rest of the book, with attention to clinical psychologists as one professional group, amongst a few, of applied human scientists.

Note

1 The Maudsley Hospital was and remains the main associate clinical base for the Institute of Psychiatry, a college of the University of London. For this reason, the hospital's name is sometimes used synonymously with that of the Institute.

2

THE KNOWLEDGE BASE OF CLINICAL PSYCHOLOGY

In the previous chapter we traced the evolution of British psychology and argued that the knowledge base of the discipline has always been contested. Like other branches of the social sciences, such as anthropology and sociology, psychology embraces a wide range of theoretical and methodological positions. However, as we have already shown, the dominant orthodoxy in British psychology is positivist and empiricist. When we begin to consider the knowledge base of *clinical* psychology in Britain, the issues become yet more complex. We are confronted with the differing agendas of the clinicians and their academic colleagues, boundary disputes between clinical psychology and other mental health professions (particularly psychiatry), and attempts by the profession to market itself successfully without giving psychology away (Rose, 1996).

Before proceeding further in our examination of clinical psychology, we will first establish a context for our discussion by examining the relationship between knowledge and the professions. Sociological analyses of the professions concur in identifying knowledge as the 'core generating trait' of professionalism (Halliday, 1987: 29). In the following section we consider the basis for this claim.

Knowledge and the professions

The emergence of the professions required a number of conditions that Polyani (1957) calls 'the great transformation'. First, knowledge had to become a socio-cultural entity that existed independently of social institutions, such as the Church. Second, the relationship between society and knowledge had to evolve in a particular manner. Finally, market forces had to develop to the extent that private provision of knowledge-based services was feasible and sustainable. Gellner (1988) explains the second point:

> ...a Nature independent of society cannot be avoided; but there is no need normally to systematize it into a single, socially independent, unified system, and indeed societies do not normally do anything of the kind. When it does happen, it constitutes a historically rare and difficult achievement. (Gellner, 1988: 51–2)

Gellner reminds us that the cognitive system that has evolved in Western society over the last 400 years is radically different from the organisation of the knowledge base that existed in earlier societies. He argues that economic development requiring manipulation of the natural world is a feature of modern society; survival was the prime concern of pre-agrarian and agrarian societies. Survival depended on group cohesion, and that required adherence to the norms of society: the repository of all received knowledge. Challenges to that received knowledge could not be sanctioned because they threatened social cohesion, and thus could endanger the group's survival. Even the large agrarian societies that existed immediately before the modern period did not develop systems of knowledge that were distinct from social institutions. The elaborate cognitive systems of tribal societies were superseded by religious orthodoxy and the clergy enjoyed almost total control over knowledge. Knowledge systems did not begin to develop independently of social institutions until the Scientific Revolution of the seventeenth century when scientists started to systematically challenge traditional beliefs. During the eighteenth century, the *philosophes* of the Enlightenment continued the elaboration of independent knowledge systems as they challenged existing views about society and morality.

> Modern society is the only society ever to live by, through and for continuous cognitive and economic growth.... Cognitive growth alone made it truly possible to follow through with the pervasive domination of a society by the market. (Gellner, 1988: 129, 131)

These changes enabled independent groups of specialists to emerge, claiming expertise in particular areas of knowledge that they could sell on the free market. Some of these groups subsequently acquired the status of *professions*.

In the previous chapter we introduced some of the competing sociological perspectives on the development of the professions. Despite substantial divergence between these accounts, contemporary sociologists generally agree that some basic characteristics distinguish the professions from other occupations:

1   Professionals provide services rather than goods.
2   Whether salaried or self-employed, professionals have higher social status than manual workers.
3   This status increases in line with the length of training the professional requires in order to practise.
4   Professionals claim to have specialist knowledge about the service they provide, and expect to define and control their roles on the basis of that knowledge.

5 Credentials recognising professionals' specialist knowledge provide members with credibility in the eyes of the state and the public (Pilgrim and Rogers, 1999).

In the case of clinical psychology, its attempt to establish itself as a fully fledged profession over the past fifty years has involved a significant lengthening of training, from an informal apprenticeship, via diplomas and master's degrees, to a three-year doctoral programme. The British Psychological Society has justified this extended training in terms of the expanding role of clinical psychologists within the NHS.

Larson (1977), who draws on the work of Weber and Marx among others, interprets the social mobility of professionals and the market control they exercise over dissemination of their specialist knowledge as the result of the 'professional project':

> Professionalization is thus an attempt to translate one order of scarce resources – special knowledge and skills – into another – social and economic rewards. To maintain scarcity implies a tendency towards monopoly: monopoly of expertise in the market, monopoly of status in a system of stratification. The focus on the constitution of professional markets leads to comparing different professions in terms of the 'marketability' of their specific cognitive resources. (Larson, 1977: xvii)

Larson's concept of the professional project implies a collective pursuit of monopoly by members of a profession: a conclusion that has been criticised by writers such as Abbott (1988) and Halliday (1987), who consider it an over-determined view of professional behaviour. Macdonald (1995) points out that many studies of professions have focused on the professional *bodies*, despite the fact that they may not always represent the views of their members and may, on occasion, have their decisions overturned by members. Macdonald gives the example of the British architectural profession as one that has been divided for most of its history. As we shall see below, the same arguably applies to British clinical psychology. However, before we turn to an examination of the disputes within clinical psychology about its work and knowledge base, let us first consider the characteristics of a profession's 'cognitive resources' that make them marketable.

Indeterminacy and professional knowledge

In an influential paper, Jamous and Peloille (1970) argued that occupations are distinguishable by their ratio of *indeterminate* and *technical knowledge* (I/T). Technical knowledge can be codified according to explicit, unambiguous rules and its transmission does not necessarily require modelling by an expert. Thus, clinical psychology trainees can read an instruction manual to learn how to instruct patients in relaxation techniques. Indeterminate knowledge, however, is implicit and defies codification or precise specification. In the words of Atkinson (1981: 110): 'The language of indetermination is a language of personal knowledge.' Jamous and Peloille propose that professions are distinguishable from other occupational groups by the former's high degree of indeterminacy. Describing the ideology of clinical medicine, they conclude that good treatment results are more readily attributed to the 'potentialities and talents' of practitioners than to 'techniques and transmissable rules' (Jamous and Peloille, 1970: 140). The authors suggest that this emphasis on the indeterminacy of knowledge allows professionals considerable autonomy and powers of self-regulation.

Recent commentators have drawn attention to limitations of the I/T ratio as a model for understanding professional work. Applying Jamous and Peloille's framework to his analysis of medical training, Atkinson (1981) argues that the I/T ratio implies a false dichotomy. Instead, he suggests, the two are inextricably interrelated, since the appropriate application of technical knowledge depends on interpretative ability: the indeterminate knowledge concerning when to apply rules that we usually refer to as 'experience'. Macdonald (1995) reminds us that Jamous and Peloille developed their framework in the 1960s after studying the French hospital system of the 1950s. He points out that both the practice of medicine and the public's expectations of professionals have changed considerably since then:

> it is difficult to see how a body of professionals could maintain their knowledge base at a high level of indeterminacy indefinitely, because they would have to acknowledge the primacy of scientific knowledge if they were to maintain their legitimacy in the modern world. (Macdonald, 1995: 165)

However Cox (1995), writing in the *Australia and New Zealand Journal of Surgery,* challenges the view that scientific knowledge is the basis for professional practice. He identifies 'clinical working knowledge' as the basis of clinical practice and proposes that the multiple sources of this knowledge are the clinician's awareness of basic scientific processes; empirical descriptions of disease; clinical experience; consultation with colleagues and common sense. Cox argues that

> Clinical practice is not, and can not, be conducted as the application of bioscience theory to clinical problems. First, clinical practice is too complex, illdefined, multifaceted and situational to be handled by applying scientific method

to its activities of diagnosis and management. Second, value judgements pervade the balancing of trade-offs in every clinical decision; but science has no calculus for handling meaning, purpose and choice of actions. (Cox, 1995: 553)

Cox concludes that *clinical practice* is worthy of study in its own right. This approach requires an analysis of how clinicians manage situations in order to achieve optimal results, given that clinical judgements are often made in the absence of reliable empirical predictive data.

The development of professional judgement is a process that a number of investigators have scrutinised. Dreyfus and Dreyfus (1986), writing about the knowledge processes involved in clinical practice, identify a sequential model of knowledge acquisition in trainee practitioners. In the first (or novice) stage, the source of knowledge is primarily external to the practitioner and practice involves the application of rules and procedures learned in academic training. By the final (or expert) stage, the source of knowledge is primarily the practitioner's own experience and this allows him/her to apply theory to practice in a manner that is appropriate to the clinical context. Commenting on this analysis, Hoshmand and Polkinghorne conclude:

> In other words, experts work with knowledge differently than do novices. It suggests that an epistemology of practicing knowledge should be based on the processes of expert practitioners, not on the deliberative procedures and theoretically derived rules that constitute the practicing knowledge of novices. (Hoshmand and Polkinghorne, 1992: 60)

The premium that this developmental model places on clinical experience reflects a similar emphasis in Freidson's earlier analysis of the 'clinical mind'. *The Profession of Medicine* (1970) contains a persuasive and insightful account of the psychological and pragmatic factors that sustain clinicians' faith in the primacy of experience. Freidson argues that clinicians are fundamentally people of *action*:

> Given a commitment to action and practical solution, in the face of ambiguity the practitioner is more likely to manifest a certain will to believe in the value of his actions than to manifest a sceptical detachment. (How could a present-day psychiatrist work if he really believed the careful studies which emphasize the unreliability of diagnosis and the undemonstrability of success of psychotherapy? And how could physicians work one, two or five centuries ago?)...One work whose work requires practical application to concrete cases simply cannot maintain the same frame of mind as the scholar or scientist: he cannot suspend action in the absence of incontrovertible evidence or be sceptical of himself, his experience, his work and its fruit. In emergencies he cannot wait for the discoveries of the future. Dealing with individual cases, he cannot rely solely on probabilities or on general concepts or principles: he must also rely on his own senses. By the nature of his work the clinician must assume responsibility for practical action, and in doing so he must rely on his concrete, clinical experience. (Freidson, 1970: 168–70)

Freidson's conclusion, that the clinician must develop '[belief] in the value of his actions...in the absence of incontrovertible evidence', leads him to assert that clinicians must not only learn to accept the uncertainty of the knowledge base they draw on, but may strategically emphasise this uncertainty:

> the practitioner is very prone to emphasize the idea of *indeterminacy or uncertainty*, not the idea of regularity or of lawful, scientific behaviour. Whether or not that idea faithfully represents actual deficiencies in available knowledge or technique it does provide the practitioner with a psychological ground from which to justify his pragmatic emphasis on first hand experience. (Freidson, 1970: 169; italics in the original)

Atkinson (1981) challenges this interpretation. He argues that the concept of 'training for uncertainty' has been over-emphasised in the literature on clinical training. In response, he observes that the clinician's reliance on personal knowledge is not reliance on his own, or colleagues', uncertainties, but reliance on the *certainty* of first hand experience.

In his recent review of the literature on professional knowledge, Macdonald accepts that the concept of indeterminacy still has limited usefulness, but suggests that the framework proposed by Abbott (1988) provides greater explanatory power. Abbott's analysis of the professions gives primacy to professional *work*, while acknowledging that abstract knowledge is the essential foundation for this activity:

> For abstraction is the quality that sets interprofessional competition apart from competition among occupations in general...only a knowledge system governed by abstractions can redefine its problems and tasks, defend them from interlopers, and seize new problems....Abstraction enables survival in the competitive system of professions. (Abbott, 1988: 9)

In Abbott's view, this abstract knowledge system allows a profession to define its tasks and establish its *jurisdiction*. However, it must also engage in 'cultural work' to ensure that clients, competitors, the state and the public accept this jurisdiction.

Knowledge and professional influence

In the preceding discussion we considered how indeterminacy may aid the professional project. Halliday (1983, 1987) argues that the success of the professional project, and hence the degree of influence the profession can exert on society, also depends on the balance between *facts* and *values* within its knowledge base. He observes that professions are *scientific* (e.g. engineering, medicine), *normative* (e.g.

law, the clergy) or *syncretic:* incorporating elements of both (e.g. the military or academic professions). Halliday contends that a profession with a scientific base can enhance its influence in some circumstances by adopting a moral tone in its pronouncements, while a normative profession can enhance its influence by casting its pronouncements in technical language. In theory, syncretic professions are likely to exert most influence on society, since they can invoke scientific authority while appearing to uphold the values of that society. However, both syncretic and normative professions may have such a broad epistemological base that their influence on society is diluted because members of the profession are pursuing a range of interests and objectives. We will argue that clinical psychology is a syncretic profession, and much of the internal conflict within the profession stems from disagreements between members about the validity and appropriateness of its scientific and normative roles.

Poststructuralist accounts of the mental health professions have emphasised their normative role. Foucault (1965) argued that the profession of psychiatry emerged to fulfil the function of moral regulation within society. However, poststructuralist analyses of psychiatry in the twentieth century (Castel et al., 1979; Armstrong, 1980; Miller and Rose, 1986) have noted that the relationship between psychiatrists and their patients has changed, because (1) psychiatry no longer operates purely within the asylum; (2) its work is no longer bound up entirely with social control; and (3) large sectors of the population have accepted a view of the individual as a psychological entity.

This psychologising of the self has resulted in individuals entering into voluntary relationships with mental health professionals and engaging in various types of 'talking treatments' in efforts to construct and reconstruct the self. Despite the voluntary nature of these relationships, the poststructuralists still stress the regulatory function of this professional enterprise:

> Correlatively, freedom has come to mean the realization of the potentials of the psychological self in and through activities in the mundane world of everyday life. The significance of psychology, here, is the elaboration of a know-how of this autonomous individual striving for self-realization. Psychology has thus participated in reshaping the practices of those who exercise authority over others – social workers, managers, teachers, nurses – such that they nurture and direct these individual strivings in the most appropriate and productive fashions.... And [psychology] has given birth to a range of psychotherapies that aspire to enabling humans to live as free individuals through subordinating themselves to a form of therapeutic authority: to live as an autonomous individual, you must learn new techniques for understanding and practising upon yourself. Freedom, that is to say, is enacted only at the price of relying upon experts of the soul. (Rose, 1996: 17)

Rose and others have noted that the language and assumptions of psychotherapy have percolated into most areas of modern life, and may be found, for example, in business, education, medicine and advertising. This has occurred because, contrary to Larson's view of the professions as seeking monopoly status, the mental health professions have been happy to give away their specialist knowledge to other professional groups, as well as to their clients. Their own heterogeneity has endowed the mental health professions with a 'peculiar penetrative capacity in relation to practices for the conduct of conduct' that has been enhanced by their 'practicable recipes for action' and apparent legitimacy as purveyors of truth about human beings (Rose, 1996: 33–4). We will consider the implications of the poststructuralist view of the psy complex in greater detail in Chapter 6.

The preceding account captures some of the tensions in the continuing debate about the knowledge base of the professions, particularly those in the clinical field. We have noted that *indeterminacy* seems to be a defining feature of professional knowledge, although there is debate about the degree of indeterminacy that is helpful to a profession in defining and defending its territory. We have also noted that professional judgement has been viewed as a source of uncertainty by some writers, and endowed with greater explanatory power than scientific theory by others. Third, we have suggested that professions survive by convincing the public and the state of the value of their specialist knowledge. Finally, we have considered some of the factors that determine how much influence a profession may exert on society.

If we consider how this debate has been conducted in relation to clinical psychology, it becomes apparent that there has been a similar tension throughout the profession's history between the abstract, theoretical knowledge base of academic psychologists and the 'clinical working knowledge' of practitioners. While clinical psychology has marketed itself as a scientific discipline, the profession has also performed a normative function, and has members who do not view themselves first and foremost as applied scientists. In the following sections we will first consider the legitimacy of psychology's claim to be science based and we will then discuss the implications of this claim for clinical psychology.

Is psychology a science?

Clinical psychology in both Britain and the USA has promoted itself as a science-based enterprise and has used this to establish its professional jurisdiction (Abbott, 1988). Before we consider the validity of the clinical psychologist as scientist-practitioner, we should acknowledge the continuing controversy within its parent discipline, psychology, over its own scientific status.

Psychology began to establish its independence from its philosophical roots during the latter part of the nineteenth century in a climate of logical positivism (see p. 8). The Vienna school of logical positivists sought to demarcate formal statements of logic from meaningful scientific statements by insisting that the latter must be verified by observation or 'protocol' statements. These protocol statements must be testable, and must therefore derive from observable physical events that could be specified in operational terms. Thus, inner experience was considered unsuitable for examination unless a physical correlate could be identified and operationally defined. The logical positivists also demanded that scientific endeavours should be logically coherent, and this necessitated a methodology of deductive reasoning based on carefully formulated hypotheses.

From the 1930s onwards, logical positivism had a significant influence on psychology, especially in the USA. All the leading behaviourists, such as Tolman, Hull and Skinner, espoused its principles. In 1939, the psychophysicist S.S. Stevens published a paper on 'Psychology and the science of science' in which he declared:

> Science seeks to generate confirmable propositions by fitting a formal system of symbols (language, mathematics, logic) to empirical observations: the propositions of science have empirical significance when their truth can be demonstrated by a set of concrete operations. (Stevens, 1939: 222)

This statement summarises the intellectual position of a generation of behaviourists. They championed hypothetico-deductive methodologies, quantification and operationism: the view promulgated by Harvard mathematician P.W. Bridgeman (1927) that concepts must be defined operationally rather than in terms of their intrinsic properties.

The role of hypothesis testing in science was developed by Popper, who began by criticising the logical positivists' emphasis on verification of hypotheses. He argued that it is possible to find empirical facts to support even the most absurd conclusions. Instead, Popper suggested the principle of falsifiability: scientific theories must be capable of predictions that are falsifiable. Following the widespread acceptance of Popper's proposal, researchers recognised that it was necessary to devise experiments that would test hypotheses by searching for data that would *not* support them. Thus, Popper provided a means for judging scientific theories: they must be (1) refutable; (2) allow for sufficient scope of observation; and (3) resist permutation into less testable versions in the presence of disconfirming data.

As we noted in Chapter 1, Hans Eysenck was one of the psychologists who believed strongly in the experimental method and the importance of hypothesis testing:

> what is needed in psychology, as in any other science, is greater understanding of and more extensive use of, the hypothetico-deductive method, in which a clear, unambiguous hypothesis is stated, deductions, preferably of a quantitative kind, are made, and experiments performed to verify or disprove the hypothesis. (Eysenck, 1952: 16)

The methodology of hypothesis testing generated a need for accurate and reliable measurement, and statistical procedures to analyse the data. The statistical work of R.A. Fisher was embraced by psychologists and his principle of the null hypothesis[1] became the foundation of experimental psychology. While logical positivism has come under increasing attack from other theoretical camps, the methodology it spawned has remained central to psychology.

In his history of modern psychology, Thomas Leahey suggests that psychology has sought recognition as a science for three reasons: (1) since human beings are part of the natural world, it appears logical that the study of human behaviour should fall within the domain of natural science; (2) scientific disciplines have been granted more status and respectability than non-scientific disciplines since the nineteenth century; and (3) scientific status was essential, particularly in the USA, to psychology's 'pretensions to social control' (Leahey, 2001: 24). However, as Leahey points out, scientific knowledge attempts to describe a world 'in which people play no part at all'; it is 'knowledge that has no point of view'. Is it possible, he asks, that there can 'be a view from nowhere – a natural science – about human beings?' (Leahey, 2001: 22–3). He concludes:

> Physics envy is a hallmark of twentieth century psychology, especially in America. Psychologists engage in a Newtonian fantasy: One day, their faith says, a Newton will arise among psychologists and propound a rigorous theory of behaviour delivering psychology unto the promised land of science. (Leahey, 2001: 24)

Jones and Elcock (2001) are among those who have argued that modern psychology is based on a misinterpretation of science as it applies to disciplines such as physics or chemistry. They base their conclusions on a number of observations that we can only summarise briefly here. Jones and Elcock note, for example, that psychologists adopted the concept of 'operational definitions' from the work of Bridgeman (1927). Behavioural psychologists, with their anti-metaphysical bias, interpreted this to mean quantification of 'objective' events, although Bridgeman's own theory of operational analysis granted equal importance to mental and physical operations. Referring to the work of Danziger (1997), Jones and Elcock argue that by adopting the 'language of variables' in a bid for scientific respectability, psychologists have forced themselves to operate within a straitjacket:

> Adopting the language of variables...as the sole language of theoretical exposition placed severe limits on what was seen as appropriate for psychological theorizing. Causality is reduced to a crude concatenation of antecedents and consequences, the complex patterns that psychology needed to deal with were reduced to lists of (logically and, necessarily for statistics) elements that were independent of each other. Part of the problem is a continuing expectation that single causes will be found for complex phenomena. It may also be the reason why psychology abounds with mini-theories rather than recognizable theoretical systems. (Jones and Elcock, 2001: 201–2)

They point out that much of psychological research is conducted on variation between individuals, while in physics there are two levels of theory: those that enhance our understanding of general principles and those that explain variation among physical phenomena. These two explanatory levels are effectively conflated in psychology and this produces theories that arguably fall short of achieving either objective satisfactorily.

Jones and Elcock proceed to make a number of technical points about the constraints of the experimental method and the limitations of statistical analyses in enhancing our understanding of human behaviour. They also note that these problems are compounded by the widespread misapplication of methodological and statistical procedures by psychologists. This point has been made by others regarding scientific research in general (see, for example, Slife and Williams, 1995; Thompson, 1999). While acknowledging that quantitative methods have a useful role in furthering psychological enquiry, they conclude by urging psychologists to adopt a critical and reflexive approach to their investigative work. In methodological terms, they encourage the use of qualitative *and* quantitative approaches. They also ask us to become more aware of the cultural context and constraints of the knowledge we are producing, and to acknowledge that 'the expertise we sell has a political and moral dimension' instead of avoiding this responsibility by subscribing to the myth of scientific objectivity (Jones and Elcock, 2001: 212).

A further criticism of 'psychology as science' concerns its relevance, rather than its validity. As we saw in the previous chapter,

British psychology developed as a scientific discipline in part as a response to the vigorous self-help culture that flourished in the first half of the twentieth century and promoted a popular psychology (Thomson, 2001). Scientific psychology attempted to improve on the popular discourse by introducing methodological and theoretical rigour to the debate. However, the methodological constraints of scientific psychology, discussed above, have limited the applicability of its theories to everyday life. Jones and Elcock conclude that 'psychology's failure to engage with everyday psychology leaves a gap which is filled by psychological discourses that often have weak theoretical and empirical bases' (2001: 197).

Similar issues have been the subject of vigorous debate among clinical psychologists. The profession, like its parent discipline, has worked hard to promote the scientific basis of its practice. This boundary work[2] has arguably been very successful in enabling the profession to establish and defend its territory within the psy complex, but the appropriateness and legitimacy of these claims continue to be contested by many of its members.

Clinical psychology and the scientist-practitioner model

As noted in the previous chapter clinical psychology emerged in a milieu dominated by the medical model. Eysenck, its most influential spokesman in the post-war period, advocated that clinical psychologists should be trained only in research and diagnostic testing, or psychometrics. In an attempt to establish clinical psychologists as independent collaborators working with (not for) psychiatrists, he strategically emphasised their research role, since testing could be delegated to technicians. This boundary work by Eysenck resulted in a tension between the role of independent scientist that he promulgated and that of scientific auxiliary, preferred by many psychiatrists. In reality, the stress on research at the Maudsley Hospital where Eysenck worked was unusual. Psychologists entering the profession in the 1950s and early 1960s to work in other institutions were generally limited to administering tests required by the psychiatrists (Derksen, 2001).

Eysenck did not consider therapeutic skills to be necessary or desirable for clinical psychologists, believing that therapy should be left to psychiatrists (Eysenck, 1949). 'Talking treatments' undertaken by psychiatrists were, at that time, primarily psychoanalytic and Eysenck viewed psychoanalysis as theoretically unsound and ineffective (Eysenck, 1952). However, it was also expedient for Eysenck to demarcate a territory for clinical psychology that did not include therapy since the psychiatrists had no intention of sharing that territory with another profession. The clinical director at the Maudsley, Aubrey Lewis, made it clear to Eysenck from the outset that independent treatment by psychologists would not be countenanced (Derksen, 2001).

During the 1940s and 1950s, Eysenck and his colleague Monte Shapiro attempted to legitimise the emerging profession of clinical psychology by emphasising the scientific underpinnings of their practice. The difficulty with this objective was, according to one of Eysenck's contemporaries, the absence of science to apply: 'It is doubtful...whether there exists what might be called a science of abnormal psychology at the present time' (Payne, 1953: 151). In the absence of suitable theory, Eysenck's team decided to adopt the experimental method in clinical work, reformulating diagnosis as a series of hypotheses to be systematically tested. Unfortunately, this approach was too time-consuming to prove useful: Payne recorded that many of their investigations took as long as a year and were both demanding of patients and delayed their treatment. Furthermore, 'Psychiatrists seldom acted on any of our recommendations' (Jones, 1984: 7).

Having reached the end of this cul-de-sac, clinical psychologists at the Maudsley began to apply the experimental method to treatment, and so behaviour therapy began to develop in Britain. Learning theory and other theories from experimental psychology were applied following the methodology developed by Monte Shapiro: the problem was defined, hypotheses were developed regarding its cause/cure, and these were then tested. The emergence of behaviour therapy enabled clinical psychologists to embrace the therapeutic role without compromising their stance as applied scientists (Pilgrim and Treacher, 1992). Furthermore, it encouraged Eysenck to extend his boundary work. In his 1958 lecture to the Royal Medico-Psychological Association, Eysenck introduced behaviour therapy to his audience of psychiatrists and claimed the neuroses as the proper territory of clinical psychologists. At the time his bid was met with hostility, but the proposal that psychiatrists concern themselves with disease processes while psychologists treat learned responses was, in fact, eventually accepted by both professions and allowed them to work in reasonable harmony for a number of years.

The Maudsley view of clinical psychology's proper role dominated clinical psychology training in Britain until the mid-1970s, because most of the courses were headed by Maudsley graduates. The dominance of the scientist-practitioner model in Britain was paralleled by similar developments in the United States. A major conference on training convened by the American Psychological Association in 1949 in Boulder, Colorado also accepted this model (henceforth known in both the USA and Britain as the 'Boulder model') as the basis for training clinical psychologists in the United States. As a result, the scientist-practitioner ideal was singularly influential in shaping both British and North American clinical psychology training during the profession's early years.

Challenges to the legitimacy of the scientist-practitioner model

During the 1970s, several factors contributed to a reaction within the profession against the Maudsley agenda of psychometrics and behaviour therapy. The growing resistance to this agenda within clinical psychology paralleled a shift in the *Zeitgeist* away from positivism and empiricism; the emergence of a new psychiatric libertarianism that implicitly challenged the conservative, scientific Maudsley tradition; and the trend towards eclecticism in other mental health professions. One expression of this resistance was the formation of the Psychology and Psychotherapy Association in 1973, founded by a group of psychologists with a broadly humanistic approach. The increasingly humanistic and eclectic ethos within the profession did not coexist easily with the Maudsley interpretation of the scientist-practitioner model. This theoretical tension had political ramifications. Clinical psychology had previously protected its occupational niche by claiming specialist science-based skills. Therefore, in order for the profession to maintain its scientific credibility, a compromise position of scientific humanism developed (Pilgrim and Treacher, 1992).

Smail (1982) describes applicants for clinical psychology training during the eclectic period as uncommitted, confused or agnostic regarding psychological theory. He suggests that they had nothing to fight for or react against. Within the profession there was no consensus about the theoretical stance or form of practice that should be identified with clinical psychology. However, despite growing interest in psychotherapy, the model of scientist-practitioner still dominated training.

Claridge and Brooks (1973) surveyed applicants to the Glasgow clinical psychology course. They found that only 12 per cent of the trainees identified strongly with the applied scientist role and were entering the profession with the intention of pursuing research. Eighty-seven per cent of the trainees identified helping and problem-solving as the most important aspects of their future role and were primarily motivated by a desire to become therapists. Claridge and

Brooks argued that university courses had two aims that were not readily compatible: vocational training to equip clinical psychologists for a role within the NHS, and academic training to maintain the scientific credibility of abnormal psychology. Pilgrim and Treacher (1992) argue that, despite some increase in flexibility in training since the study by Claridge and Brooks, the role of clinical psychologist as researcher has not developed adequately in line with the scientist-practitioner model.

Some commentators within the profession have concluded that the model of scientist-practitioner is no longer tenable in Britain or the USA. O'Sullivan and Dryden (1990) surveyed clinical psychologists in the South-East Thames region and found that research was the least frequent activity, filling only 6 per cent of their time. Other studies support the conclusion that research does not fit easily into the schedule of an NHS clinician confronted by the pressures of waiting lists (Agnew et al., 1995; Skinner, 1996; Jefferis et al., 1997). Similar findings have been reported in the USA, and on both sides of the Atlantic a very small proportion of the profession produces the research. Most of these individuals are relatively senior, and many are affiliated with academic centres.

In response to these findings, some writers have suggested reconsidering the type of research that clinicians might usefully and feasibly complete in order to bridge the gap between scientist and practitioner. Thus, small N designs, 'quick and dirty' research, and projects based on routine clinical work are advocated instead of more theoretical studies which require large Ns and well-controlled variables (Milne, 1987; Paxton, 1987; Spellman and Ross, 1987). Head and Harmon (1991) have argued the opposing view, asserting that these proposals amount to a double standard within the profession, with rigour demanded during training and dispensed with after qualification.

The Mowbray Report: renewed legitimacy for the scientist-practitioner model

Despite indications that its influence may be limited, the scientist-practitioner model has persisted in the self-presentation of the profession. It has done so because the model is an essential feature of the identity projected by clinical psychologists in order to differentiate themselves from psychiatrists, nurses, social workers and other therapists. Over the past ten years the boundary work of clinical psychologists has been assisted in this respect by the findings of the Mowbray Report.

As noted in Chapter 1, Mowbray concluded that only clinical psychologists possess level 3 skills: the ability, as applied scientists, to problem-solve using a broad base of psychological knowledge. This conclusion proved opportune for expansionists within the profession as they sought new roles for clinical psychologists, particularly in the field of primary care. The 'level 3' argument has been used extensively, for example in boundary work delineating the respective roles of clinical psychologists and community psychiatric nurses:

> Community psychiatric nurses cannot do what we can do...what we should be doing is saying that we can tackle problems that do not have standardised solutions. We can think through from first principles in ways that other professionals cannot. Our strength, which we have got to get across, is that we are special because we combine knowledge of a wider client group, with knowledge about clinical skills, with knowledge about psychological theories. Other professions may be skilled in one of these three areas, but only clinical psychologists can combine all three. (Parry, 1990, cited in Pilgrim, 1990)

Parry's emphasis on the special skills psychologists use to *combine* different types of knowledge exemplifies Abbott's claim that abstraction defines professional knowledge and enables professions to defend their territory (Abbott, 1988). However, successful boundary work requires adaptation to meet new challenges. In Chapter 5 we will discuss how clinical psychology is currently redefining its scientist-practitioner model as 'evidence-based practitioner' in order to retain its territory.

Conclusions

In this chapter we have considered the knowledge base of clinical psychology. We have described how its parent discipline allied itself with the natural sciences in a bid to differentiate itself from popular psychology, on the one hand, and philosophy on the other. In a similar way, clinical psychology has sought respectability through its promotion of the scientist-practitioner model, and has used this to establish credibility with the medical profession while simultaneously distancing itself from (and attempting to elevate itself above) therapists of diverse backgrounds in an increasingly competitive field. A recent remark in an editorial by an eminent Scottish psychiatrist is an indication of the success of the profession's boundary work:

> It is not difficult, therefore, to visualise a scenario in which an increasingly large and self-confident profession of clinical psychology, equipped with doctorate

degrees, consultant titles and a wide range of therapeutic skills of proven efficacy, might seem before long, to both general practitioners and to the health departments, to be the most important source of therapeutic skills and professional advice in the mental health field. (Kendell, 2000: 9)

The scientist-practitioner concept has proved to have enduring market value and is currently demonstrating its worth in a climate of clinical governance and evidence-based medicine.

Despite the success of clinical psychology's professional project, not all of its members are persuaded by the justificatory rhetoric that surrounds this enterprise. Smail (2001) claims that there is a 'distortion of truth by interest' as we protect our professional territory:

> In the case of psychotherapy, our blinkered pursuit of our professional interest and our obsession with shoring up our credentials and refining a rhetoric of credibility has taken us up a blind alley in which we are no longer able to discern the real features of our undertaking. In fact, we have not really got a clue what constitutes good psychotherapy, not because the question is unanswerable but because we steadfastly refuse to pose it in an appropriate way. We insist on there being only certain kinds of answer to this question, i.e. those which conform to our notion of psychotherapy as trainable, quasi-medical technique. When we perceive the answers which begin to take shape as we research our activities, we panic and retreat into denial. (Smail, 2001: 16)

Smail is urging us not to discount the personal and relational nature of psychotherapy, nor the social context of our work. His remarks about answers being constrained by the sort of questions we ask resonate with the argument of Jones and Elcock (2001) summarised above, in which they claimed that the 'language of variables' has forced psychologists to operate within a straitjacket. Smail continues:

> In contrast with the largely specious picture shaped almost exclusively by our interest in developing a marketable product, we are presented with a view of psychotherapy as a quintessentially human undertaking full of uncertainty, frailty even, in which a kind of healing may emerge, perhaps, from the exquisitely vulnerable endeavours of two people acting in the best faith they can muster. (Smail, 2001: 17)

We retreat here from the model of evidence-based practitioner and return to contemplate the indeterminacy of professional knowledge. In Smail's description, the work of the clinical psychologist does not sound like application of scientific theory.

Clinical psychology is a segmented profession. It is segmented through divisions into clinical specialities, different work settings and by its members' adherence to different models of therapy/ treatment. More fundamental still is the lack of consensus on the nature of clinical psychology, whether or not it is truly a scientific enterprise and, if so, how that might be defined. Dispute about this issue has wide-ranging implications for the profession's self-presentation and identification of its legitimate role in society. We will return to these questions in Chapter 7.

Notes

1 The *null hypothesis* states that data resulting from an experiment are *not* due to the effects of an independent variable, or a correlation between variables, as predicted by an *experimental hypothesis*.

2 Gieryn (1999) defines boundary work as the largely rhetorical activity that practitioners pursue to demarcate their area of expertise and exclude unwanted participants.

3

CLINICAL PSYCHOLOGY TRAINING

In this chapter we will describe how one becomes a clinical psychologist in Britain. The chapter is divided into three: the first section provides an account of the experience of training from the trainees' perspective; the second section covers current training arrangements; and the third section outlines recent proposals for expanding training provision. The first section, describing the experience of assistant psychologists and trainee clinical psychologists during the mid-1990s, will highlight some of the problems in the training system that are now being addressed through these proposed changes.

At present, the usual route to becoming a clinical psychologist in Britain has three stages: completion of an undergraduate psychology degree; a period of 'relevant' work experience after graduation; and, finally, completion of a doctoral degree in clinical psychology. It generally takes at least seven years to negotiate this passage: three years for the undergraduate degree (in Scotland this takes an additional year), a year of work experience (typically working as an assistant to a qualified clinical psychologist), and then three years of post-graduate work. In reality, it often takes longer, as individuals may continue gaining work experience for two or three years (sometimes more) while they reapply for clinical training. For many years there have been substantially more applicants than training places: hence the delays introduced by this bottleneck. We will return to this problem below, since the dearth of training places has been the catalyst for recent proposals to restructure clinical training in Britain. First, however, we will consider how this protracted passage through training is experienced by aspiring clinical psychologists.

The passage through clinical training: trainee perspectives

The following account derives from the doctoral thesis of one of the present authors, which examined the professional socialisation of clinical psychology trainees (Cheshire, 2000).

Jacox defines professional socialisation as the

process by which a person acquires the knowledge, skills and sense of occupational identity that are characteristic of a member of that profession. It involves the internalization of the values and norms of the group into the person's own behaviour and self-conception. (Jacox, 1973: 6)

The study in part reported here investigated the experiences of psychology assistants; first, second and third year trainees; and newly qualified psychologists. Between 1995 and 1999 interviews were conducted with 100 per cent (N = 39) of three consecutive intakes to the University of Edinburgh/East of Scotland Doctorate in Clinical Psychology (D. Clin. Psychol.) course. Some of the findings with more than local significance are summarised below.

The experiences of assistant psychologists

One area of investigation in this study was the degree of professional socialisation that occurs *before* individuals begin clinical training. As noted above, most courses expect candidates to acquire 'relevant experience' over a period of 1–2 years before applying, and this period is often extended because training places are limited. We would therefore expect the process of professional socialisation to be well under way before individuals enter their doctoral programmes, particularly when the 'relevant experience' has been acquired in NHS clinical psychology departments.

The respondents in this study had demonstrated commitment to the profession, in terms of work experience and academic choices, over periods ranging from one to eleven years before commencing formal training. The majority (67 per cent) first considered clinical psychology as a future career during their undergraduate degree: typically, this occurred in the third or fourth year. A further eight individuals (20 per cent) first contemplated this career while at secondary school. The least common route to clinical training involved a relatively late career choice, following completion of an undergraduate degree.

Assistants' views of clinical psychology are one indicator of their professional socialisation. The majority were sufficiently positive about the profession to pursue clinical training, but were critical of aspects of its practice and self-presentation. Some of these individuals expressed concerns about the signs of burn-out they had observed among qualified psychologists and were already thinking about how to protect themselves post-qualification by combining clinical work with different options. Others questioned aspects of the profession's rhetoric that they had learned for the selection interviews for the clinical doctorates. Respondents were fairly evenly split between advocates and critics of the scientist-practitioner model. Among the critics, some were ambivalent about the model itself and saw it as incompatible with the humanistic approach they wished to adopt in their own practice. Others accepted the model as a desirable one for clinical psychologists to emulate but were sceptical about how much it influenced the practice of qualified practitioners. Most interviewees demonstrated considerable awareness of the territorial disputes between clinical psychology and other mental health professions, particularly psychiatry and nursing. Their own experience as assistants, working in varying proximity to other health professionals while trying to define their own role, had encouraged most of them to reflect on these professional issues.

Nearly half the respondents reported difficulties in their psychology assistant posts, arising from a combination of heavy workloads, role ambiguity and inadequate supervision. None of these individuals had been sufficiently disenchanted by such experiences to abandon the goal of clinical psychology training; instead they managed to preserve a favourable view of the profession by convincing themselves that their circumstances were exceptional. Some individuals not only struggled to define their roles for themselves, but also faced the challenge of defining it for non-psychologist colleagues. One assistant, for example, was the only psychologist in a multidisciplinary team, while some respondents described working with members of other professions (particularly nurses) without another psychologist on site. In these situations, individuals often found it very difficult to define their role at even a basic level. As one woman commented: 'I found it difficult to see how [my work] was psychological...I didn't know what was expected, there was nobody else there to tell me.'

When supervision was inadequate, assistants not only experienced role ambiguity, but found it difficult, if not impossible, to establish theory–practice links. For clinical psychology trainees, like psychiatry trainees (Bucher et al., 1969), there is considerable discontinuity between their undergraduate knowledge base and the instruction they receive as postgraduates. They are therefore particularly reliant on clinical supervisors to demonstrate skills and make the theory–practice links explicit. Unfortunately, some assistants were only able to make sense of the work they had been asked to do in these posts once they began the D. Clin. Psychol. and were introduced to theoretical models through the course. Here, a respondent describes her reaction to a lecture early in the course:

It was really funny today...there was somebody talking about anger management in learning disabilities and I realised I spent 8 months working with someone in anger management as an assistant, and it didn't actually strike home to me that I'd been working in a cognitive way with her. Ridiculous as that sounds, I didn't really make the links properly, yet that's what I was doing.

Her inability to identify the theoretical basis for her work as an assistant made it impossible for her to establish appropriate therapeutic goals and assess outcome.

In summary, the respondents in this study entered clinical training with considerable awareness of the rhetoric surrounding the profession's self-presentation, together with scepticism about the basis for some of its claims. This scepticism reflected their own experience of role ambiguity and their uncertainty about the reality and desirability of the scientist-practitioner model.

Starting the clinical doctorate

Most of the trainees found the transition to clinical training challenging in ways they had not anticipated. Although the majority of respondents experienced the transition to trainee status as a positive step towards a desired goal, for some it meant a drop in income and/or status that left them feeling deskilled and disempowered. Interviewees often spoke of feeling 'drained' when describing their early clinical placements and attributed this to both the intellectual and emotional demands of their clinical role. As one person said: 'sometimes you think "…my God, what can I possibly offer?" You feel overwhelmed with this suffering'. Even individuals who had done a reasonable amount of clinical work as psychology assistants acknowledged that they had been unprepared for these demands. Typically they explained their response to the transition in terms of the higher volume of clinical work they encountered as trainees, coupled with the greater complexity of the cases, increased responsibility and the rise in their expectations of themselves.

Trainees' personal responses to clinical work

Uncertainty about 'what to do' in clinical sessions appeared to be the main stressor for trainees early in the course. One first year trainee remarked:

I was panicking about the prospect of seeing patients and not having any sort of recipe book to follow…I didn't realise perhaps how much of what I've done before and what I know myself that I would have to bring.

This uncertainty gave rise to the greatest anxiety as well as frustration and disappointment in the early stages of the course because of trainees' expectations that the course would 'answer everything'.

These new trainees frequently alluded to themselves as 'pretend psychologists' and expressed concern about being exposed as novices by their patients.

By the time trainees began their second year of clinical training, most were beginning to believe a little more in themselves as 'real psychologists'. They were also becoming more confident about their ability to interview patients and conceptualise their difficulties. While 'being in charge' and 'taking control' were dominant themes in interviews with first year trainees, 'being flexible', 'being relaxed with patients' and 'trusting one's own judgement' became more important themes in the second year.

While the theme of flexibility in the application of theory to practice first emerged in the interviews with second year trainees, it dominated the accounts of third year trainees as they described their attempts to 'think about people more as individuals'. Another theme that characterised the interviews with that cohort was the necessity of accepting the ambiguity and complexity of clinical work, as this person explains:

> ...there are some people that I see that it's very hard to measure what you're doing but you know something's going on...I suppose it's just as you do go on in the profession and you get different kinds of cases, you realise how everything's not as black and white as you thought it was when you started, and it's not all about doing cognitive therapy, it's all much more complicated than that.

Other third year trainees spoke of attending more to the dynamics of the therapeutic relationship. Few of them felt confident about their ability to interpret these dynamics and a third commented that the absence of personal therapy or adequate opportunities for guided self-reflection in their training left them ill-equipped to do so.

The consensus view of the interviewees was that the third year of training had allowed them to begin consolidating the learning of the previous two years, as this respondent explains:

> At the beginning of third year I thought, 'I don't need this third year. I really don't feel as though I need any more experience. I've done as much as I can.' But you really do need it, and I think at the end of it now, the experience of doing the thesis, and you really take off, I think, confidence-wise, in the third year. I'm totally different now than I was at the end of second year I think, and I found it really came together for me in third year.

When they spoke about their increased self-confidence, some of the third year trainees explained this in terms of their belief in the value of their work. One respondent reported having 'much more of a purpose in my life now', while another commented: 'I don't want to appear precious about the profession but it is, you know, it is an incredibly important thing you're doing.'

Trainees' views of the profession

The uncertainty about the validity of the scientist-practitioner model expressed by respondents at the beginning of the D. Clin. Psychol. was still evident in the attitudes of the third year trainees. They also spoke of confusion about their professional identity. One remarked that 'there doesn't really seem to be any coherent sense of what clinical psychology is or what we should be doing', while another spoke of the 'insecurity' in clinical psychology: '…it's people trying to prove that they're good enough at the job because the status is sort of uncertain still and I think as a profession we're not exactly sure what we do'.

In addition to their concerns about their own effectiveness and the ambiguities of their professional role, a quarter of those interviewed at the end of their training expressed apprehension about the prospect of burn-out in their future careers. They based this concern on the behaviour that they had witnessed among qualified psychologists. The following response is typical:

> …being very assertive, I think, is quite important. Certainly, a lot of departments I've worked in, there's a culture of martyrdom, people working ridiculous hours and trying to get through ridiculous waiting lists, which I think, well, it's a bottomless pit in some ways. You're not going to, so that's my attitude very much. I'm not prepared to run myself down physically, mentally, whatever, so I'm going to be useless anyway.

While this respondent planned to resist 'the pressure to take on everything and everybody that comes your way', others had already considered making a time-limited commitment to the profession to protect themselves from burn-out.

Opportunities and constraints in clinical training

Once they started the D. Clin. Psychol., trainees shared a sense of entitlement about what the course should deliver. As one individual explained: 'There's the feeling that you have to be wonderful and excellent to get on the course and when you do, you expect to find out the answers to everything.' These expectations are driven by trainees' awareness of how much they have to learn: '…it's your training, it's your one chance to try and get yourself in a position of being a useful practitioner'. Since they embark on their professional training with these expectations, it is not surprising that trainees take an increasingly active part in shaping that experience. Respondents in this study shaped it collectively in various ways: for example, they requested and achieved changes to the examination timetable and teaching programme. Individually, trainees also influenced the process: for example, they exercised varying degrees of influence over the choice of research and clinical supervisors. Indeed, those with 'insider knowledge' of the system from their days as psychology assistants in departments affiliated with the course privately planned some of their clinical placements with qualified psychologists whom they knew before they began the course.

Throughout the study there was ample evidence of trainees behaving as 'active, choice-making factors in their own socialization' (Olesen and Whittaker, 1968). However, individuals also had to contend with instances of role conflict and role ambiguity. Role conflict most frequently arose from trainees' dual status as NHS employees and university postgraduates. Respondents identified much more strongly with their employee role than they did with the student role; nevertheless, they had to cope with switching between the two. In the third year, particularly, the role of student and clinician compete for the trainee's time and attention, as the trainee works on his/her dissertation while completing the final year placements.[1] This often left trainees feeling guilty about letting patients and NHS colleagues down. While trainees did value the academic component of the course, the majority attached more value to their clinical work. In practical terms this meant economy of effort in examinations and written assessments, with the exception of their case studies. Most trainees considered these to have greater value than other assessment exercises for the development of their clinical skills.

Kahn et al. (1964) identify insufficient or misleading feedback from supervisors as one source of role ambiguity, and many of the respondents in this study were critical of both university and NHS staff in this respect. In terms of their academic work, trainees complained that feedback on their written work was delayed and insufficiently detailed. This left trainees feeling uncertain about their academic proficiency and encouraged them to react defensively and devalue this aspect of the course. Trainees also reported that their clinical supervisors were often not transparent regarding the theoretical (or a-theoretical) foundations of their work. Particularly during the first two years of training, this theory–practice gap left trainees feeling confused and disorientated, while their own insecurities generally inhibited them from asking, if the information was not offered. They reported that this lack of clarity in supervision was often compounded by inadequate feedback about their own interventions.

The majority of trainees said that they would have liked more direct observation of their work and more detailed constructive criticism of their clinical skills. The consensus view was that their clinical supervisors often assumed, without sufficient evidence, that the trainees were delivering competent therapy. Trainees believed that this assumption sometimes produced an overly casual approach from supervisors because of their 'expectation that everyone's going to get on fine'. This typically increased trainees' own anxieties about their competence and led them to devalue the positive feedback they did receive from supervisors because, as one individual explained: '...at the end of three years, I don't really think that anybody really knows what I'm like as a psychologist'.

Commentary

In their study of professional socialisation of biochemists, psychiatrists and medical internists, Bucher and Stelling (1977) concluded that the experience of mastery is essential if trainees are to develop a professional identity and commitment to their profession. In this study of professional socialisation of clinical psychologists, it was apparent that assistant psychologists and clinical psychology trainees did indeed develop an increasing sense of professional mastery through direct experience of clinical work. The principal factors that constrained individuals' experience of mastery were (1) role conflict arising from trainees' combined student–employee role; and (2) role ambiguity reflecting both trainees' uncertainty about the role of the clinical psychologist and a perceived lack of transparency on the part of academic and clinical supervisors.

However, if we examine this lack of transparency in the supervisor–supervisee relationship, it is fair to say that it reflects wariness on both sides. If we consider the relationships between trainees and clinical supervisors in particular, the latter are often reluctant to give trainees negative feedback, especially in the early stages of training, in case they inadvertently undermine them. This circumspection is often matched by trainees' reluctance to disclose their own difficulties in case they are negatively evaluated. Such wariness on the part of trainees is understandable given the power relationship between trainee and supervisor. However, when this is considered together with the general reluctance of these respondents to use the support systems provided by the course,[2] their behaviour may also indicate socialisation into 'a defended professional ethos in which personal needs are perceived as detracting from the current professional climate and are therefore devalued' (Walsh and Cormack, 1994: 106). This ethos, which is also characteristic of medicine and nursing (Handy, 1991; Menzies, 1977; Payne and Firth, 1987), is unfortunately pervasive within the NHS. At the same time, the comments of some trainees about the dangers of professional burn-out suggest that those individuals intend to resist the 'culture of martyrdom' that denies these personal needs.

If we look further into the question of transparency in clinical supervision, it becomes apparent that we are again confronting questions about the indeterminacy of professional knowledge. Some clinical psychologists favour a move towards more proscriptive treatment protocols to deliver evidence-based treatment (see Chapter 5) while others continue to promote a flexible response to individual clients. Although the latter group has been criticised by the former for valuing 'mystery over mastery' (Gambril, 1990, cited in Long and Hollin, 1997: 77), their support for the indeterminacy of professional knowledge is consistent with the rhetoric about level 3 skills used by the leadership to promote clinical psychology within the NHS. It is also in line with the view of non-psychologists who identify 'clinical working knowledge' as the basis of professional practice (see Chapter 2). Against this background of vigorous debate about the appropriate knowledge base for clinical practice, trainees try to learn their craft. However, it is arguable that they are likely to experience the indeterminacy of their knowledge base as more problematic than senior members of the profession, who may value the opportunities it confers.

From their accounts, it is evident that the relationship between theory and practice is *not* always clear to trainees. It would be unfair and misleading to present this finding as though it is simply attributable to substandard clinical supervision, given the lack of consensus within the profession about that relationship and the continuing support from many psychologists (and members of other professions) for the principle of indeterminacy. Instead, trainees' experiences of the 'theory–practice dilemma' are examples of 'trouble' they will experience during their professional socialisation that is both unavoidable and potentially productive (Bucher and Stelling, 1977). By confronting this dilemma, trainees may begin to form their own responses to the continuing debate within the profession concerning its knowledge base.

In summary, the questions raised by these respondents about the validity of the scientist-practitioner model and the central task of clinical psychology (Mollon, 1989) reflect continuing debates within the profession. Many qualified practitioners who are coping with role changes within a rapidly changing NHS echo the confusion over professional identity expressed by assistant psychologists and trainees. Clinical psychology is an increasingly segmented profession, with a growing number of subdivisions representing different client groups and different theoretical orientations (see Chapters 4 and 5). The challenge for clinical training courses is to reflect this diversity and avoid the promotion of a defensive orthodoxy.

In the following sections we will first provide an overview of the current training requirements.[3] We will then consider some of the challenges facing the profession that have necessitated a review of these arrangements. Finally, we will summarise some of the alternative models of training that are presently under discussion as possible solutions to these challenges.

Clinical psychology training: current provisions

Clinical psychology is a very young profession: the Division of Clinical Psychology was not established within the British Psychological Society until 1965. Despite its youth, it has grown exponentially in size and influence over the past fifty years although it remains small when compared with most of the other health professions.[4] As the role of the clinical psychologist has grown within the Health Service, the training requirements for entry to the profession have become increasingly demanding. The training courses that were founded during the 1960s and 1970s were generally university based and awarded master's degrees as the clinical qualification. NHS in-service courses that awarded BPS diplomas were also established in the late 1960s as a stopgap until more university courses came on stream. In-service courses have now been superseded by university-based/administered courses. These courses operate in partnership with NHS Trusts, which provide the clinical placements for the trainees and fund the training places. Over the past fifteen years the courses have made the transition from two-year master's programmes to three-year doctoral degrees.

University-based practitioner doctorates

There are 31 clinical psychology training courses in the British Isles: 25 in England, two in Wales, two in Scotland, one in Northern Ireland and one in Eire. Only one of these courses (University of Hull) offers entry at undergraduate level through the UCAS system. While the Hull course consists of a six-year integrated BSc/ Doctorate in Clinical Psychology, the remaining clinical psychology training courses are three year full-time doctorates (with the University of Leeds continuing to offer both an MSc and a D. Clin. Psychol., with the expectation that most trainees will complete the doctorate). Most applications to the clinical psychology doctoral programmes are processed by the Clearing House for Postgraduate Courses in Clinical Psychology (CHPCCP).[5] The Clearing House is a non-profit educational charity managed by a committee of representatives from the Group of Trainers in Clinical Psychology and the Affiliates Group of the Division of Clinical Psychology. It is financed entirely by the application fees and is based at the University of Leeds.

The postgraduate courses vary in size: in 2001, there were 454 training places in total (range 8-32 per course).[6] This represents a substantial increase in recent years (compared with, for example, 263 in 1995); the total number is expected to continue rising in response to growing demand for psychological services in the NHS. Although demand for training places continues to outstrip supply, the odds for prospective candidates are improving due to an increase in training places and a slight fall in the number of applicants over the past five years. In 1995, there were 1,398 applicants for clinical training through the Clearing House Scheme and 263 (19 per cent) were successful. The number of applicants peaked the following year (totalling 1,645), with 18 per cent achieving places, but by 2001 applicants had fallen to 1,486, with 31 per cent gaining places. Possible explanations for the decline in numbers include: the growing number of alternative careers, such as health, forensic and counselling psychology; the move towards registration of psychotherapists (see Chapter 1) that will provide another path towards professional legitimacy for therapists; the historical difficulties of obtaining a clinical psychology training place; and the 'embeddedness' of training in the NHS, which precludes psychologists working in non-NHS settings (such as industry or the prison service) from applying (Edelmann, 2001).

Most of the doctoral programmes in clinical psychology demand that applicants have a 2:1 or a First in a BA/BSc Psychology Honours degree, which confers eligibility for the BPS Graduate Basis for Registration. A few will consider candidates with a 2:2 in 'exceptional circumstances', although they may expect those candidates to complete a Master's degree (for example, in research methods) before they apply for clinical training. In addition to a good first degree, candidates for clinical training are generally required to show that they have acquired 'relevant experience' prior to application. Very few courses will consider applications from undergraduates.

Given these prerequisites for clinical training, trainees are typically in their mid to late twenties when they train, although a significant proportion enter training in their thirties or later.

Many individuals begin to acquire this relevant work experience before they finish their undergraduate degree: for those who have chosen their career path early, the experience may have been carefully planned, while for others it is initially serendipitous. A wide range of work experience is likely to satisfy selectors on the doctoral courses, as long as it represents experience of working with people and provides some opportunity for application of psychological knowledge. The *Clearing House Handbook* explains that 'relevant clinically related experience...helps to establish that applicants know what they are applying for, what clinical psychologists do, the settings they work in, and the people they work with' (2002: 138). Much of this experience is gained within the voluntary sector, or through employment in positions such as nursing assistants, paid carers and psychology assistants within departments of clinical psychology. Clinical research also provides suitable work experience.

The clinical psychology training courses are accredited by the BPS through the Committee on Training in Clinical Psychology (CTCP), which organises inspections of the courses every five years. In order to remain accredited, the courses must satisfy criteria established by the CTCP, as well as criteria for the award of doctoral degrees established by the universities linked to the courses. As a result, the courses vary little in structure and content. They are required to provide training in four core clinical areas: work with adults; children and adolescents; people with learning disabilities; and older adults. In addition, trainees are expected to receive some 'specialist' experience. This covers options such as forensic work, neuropsychology, and working in general medical settings. Specialist placements also include more advanced training in particular therapies, or training in an alternative approach. The courses are required to provide supervised experience in more than one therapeutic approach.

Trainees spend at least 50 per cent of their time acquiring clinical experience. The remainder of their time is divided between academic work and research activity. The courses are expected to teach research methodology (building on undergraduate foundations) and trainees are required to have experience of small-scale service-orientated research in at least one placement. Furthermore, they must 'report formally' on a larger-scale piece of clinically relevant research.

The *Clearing House Handbook* states:

Training courses seek to produce professionally qualified Clinical Psychologists eligible for Chartered Status,[7] for employment in the National Health Service, and also in clinical research, clinical academic teaching and in developing the range of service applications for clinical psychology. (2002: 5)

The stated purpose of the training courses is reflected in funding arrangements. Successful applicants are employed as trainee clinical psychologists by an NHS Trust that is affiliated with their training course. Salaries are paid according to Whitley Council trainee clinical psychology pay scales (£15,185–£17,078 in 2002).[8] The NHS currently provides enough funding for all available training places, so opportunities for individuals to self-fund training through scholarships or grants from overseas governments are unlikely at present. Equally, NHS-funded places are unlikely to be offered to overseas applicants. While some courses merely state that they are training people to work in the NHS, others state that preference will be given to individuals who demonstrate commitment to working post-qualification in the geographical area served by the funding NHS Trust(s). A few courses stipulate in their training contract that successful applicants will be expected to seek employment locally for a specified period after qualification – usually two years.

From 1 April 1999 the funding for the two Scottish training courses has been co-ordinated centrally through the Scottish Council for Postgraduate Medical and Dental Education (SCPMDE). In April 2002 a new Special Health Board (NHS Education for Scotland: NES) was established to combine governance of SCPMDE, the National Board for Nursing, Midwifery and Health Visiting (NBS) and the Post-Qualification Board for Pharmacists in Scotland (PQBP) (see p. 59 below).

Statements of Equivalence from the British Psychological Society

The Statement of Equivalence in Clinical Psychology (SoE) is the other route towards becoming a chartered clinical psychologist in Britain. The SoE is a procedure that allows clinical psychologists who have trained overseas, or psychologists from other specialities (such as counselling or educational psychology), to gain recognition for their qualifications from the BPS. The Committee for the Scrutiny of Individual Clinical Qualifications (CSICQ) awards the SoE and adopts the UK clinical training model as its benchmark. CSICQ assesses applicants by comparing their qualifications with the training requirements that existed in the UK at the time that they trained, although post-qualification experience is also considered.

Applicants who cannot demonstrate 'equivalence' in their training are asked to complete further academic, clinical or research work before the SoE is awarded. Only about 15 per cent of applicants are awarded the SoE without completing further training (McGuire et al., 2001).

Full-time clinical psychology doctorates and the SoE are currently the only systems in place for training and credentialing clinical psychologists in Britain. We will now consider recent proposals designed to increase the flexibility and effectiveness of existing training provisions.

The future of clinical psychology training in Britain

The National Service Framework for Mental Health (Department of Health, 1999a) emphasises the need for an expanding workforce that will be responsive to the needs of a modernising NHS. Within this framework, funding for training 1,000 graduate mental health workers in primary care and 500 'gateway' community mental health workers (probably recruited from community psychiatric nursing and social work) is expected to become available in 2003–4 (Department of Health, 2001b). The first group will be trained in 'brief evidence-based effective interventions' for 'common mental disorders'. In addition to direct work with clients, these primary care workers will be expected to become involved in health promotion, audit, and the development of links between primary care and other statutory and non-statutory services. The Workforce Action Team Report states that applicants for these posts will be graduates in a 'relevant discipline' and 'graduate psychologists will be in a strong position to apply' (Department of Health, 2001b). Furthermore, the Report notes that clinical psychologists will play a key role in the supervision of these primary care workers. Cognitive-behaviour therapists, health psychologists and counselling psychologists are already in post in some parts of the country, joining forces with clinical psychologists within departments of clinical psychology. Some of these skill-mix models have been carefully planned, but more often they reflect a failure to recruit enough clinical psychologists to fill available posts.

Against this background, debates about training within clinical psychology are focusing on how to expand the profession as rapidly as possible to meet the ever-increasing demand for psychological services. Proposals to increase the flexibility of training have addressed three areas of concern: (1) the under-utilisation/exploitation of assistant psychologists; (2) inefficiencies in the Statement of Equivalence system; and (3) the dearth of doctoral training places. We will summarise recent proposals pertaining to each of these areas below.

The training of assistant psychologists

In January 1998, the Division of Clinical Psychology published official guidelines for the employment of assistant psychologists. The guidelines were intended to protect assistants from various forms of exploitation and mismanagement reported in a number of studies. These studies concluded that some assistant psychologists received inadequate training, supervision and support but were reluctant to complain about their working conditions in case this jeopardised their future prospects (Harper and Newton, 1988; Harper 1990; Rezin and Tucker, 1998).

The guidelines for the employment of assistant psychologists stipulate that assistants must be professionally accountable to and receive supervision from a qualified clinical psychologist. They also define appropriate roles for assistants: they should not substitute for qualified clinicians; substitute for clerical or care assistants; work in the absence of 'highly competent supervision'; or take on inappropriately complex clinical tasks. Assistants should be given a written induction pack and a minimum of a fortnight's induction period, followed by a staged introduction to the work. Finally, the guidelines provide for a minimum of a half-day per week for private study and a minimum of an hour's supervision per week, with detailed recommendations for the content of supervision (Division of Clinical Psychology, 1998).

Gallagher and Brosnan (2001) investigated adherence to the guidelines in a survey of assistant psychologists. They found that this continues to vary between posts and departments, but the authors were encouraged to discover that most of the respondents were satisfied with the amount of supervision and support they were receiving. Respondents did identify a need for more formalised training in many assistant posts.

Miller and Wilson (1998) argue that the profession makes poor use of assistants' potential to contribute to psychology services that are now increasingly based on a skill-mix model. They accept the DCP guidelines as the necessary first step in improving the situation, but suggest that additional measures need to be taken. These measures include: the development of minimum training standards for assistants; extension of pay scales to overlap with those of trainee clinical psychologists;[9] access by assistants to some of the academic modules on the doctoral training courses; and clearer guidelines from the training courses about how selectors assess 'clinically relevant training', given that the vast majority of assistants are future applicants. As we explain in our discussion of postgraduate training in clinical psychology below, the idea of greater continuity between the training of assistants and that offered to trainee clinical psychologists has also been explored in other arenas.

Training for the statement of equivalence

The Statement of Equivalence system has been criticised on several grounds. At present, applicants have to find their own training co-ordinator and supervisor. This is quite a complicated business for new arrivals in the country and is likely to be an unnecessarily protracted affair. Once individuals begin working for the SoE they can expect varying degrees of support from their employers, ranging from provision of placements on full pay to unpaid day release for placement work. Candidates for the SoE often have little or no contact with each other and the experience can be stressful and isolating. In 1997–8 only two-thirds of the psychologists who sat examinations for the SoE were successful at the first attempt. The assessment procedures for the SoE have been criticised for failing to take account of the candidates' prior experience, being excessively rigorous relative to the doctoral courses, and lacking adequate appeals procedures (Lund, 2002; Willner and Napier, 2001). There are likely to be about 100 individuals working for the NHS at any one time who are completing further training for the SoE (McGuire et al., 2001). This places considerable demands on NHS clinical psychologists, who supervise applicants, and on members of the CSICQ and related BPS committees, who assess applicants and administer the SoE.

At a mini-conference on the SoE in January 2000, a number of suggestions were made for improving the current training and assessment system. It was proposed that co-ordination and examination for the SoE should be handed over to the clinical training courses, and it was also suggested that the SoE should be linked to a doctoral qualification so that these candidates could eventually achieve true equivalence (see also Willner and Napier, 2001). Other proposals included the formalising of the training co-ordinator's role through a remunerated contract of employment, and more detailed information for candidates about the assessment procedures, placements, supervisors and training co-ordinators. In response to these concerns, a co-ordinated SoE scheme is currently being piloted for candidates in south-east London, Kent and East Sussex (Whittington and Burns, 2001) and further reforms of the

SoE system are likely. The continuing dearth of clinical psychologists will undoubtedly drive these reforms, given that the SoE candidates can often complete their additional training requirements within two years, compared with the three year doctoral courses of the mainstream trainees.

Postgraduate training in clinical psychology

The criteria for accreditation of post-graduate training courses in clinical psychology have been amended many times over the years, and they are currently under review once again. Towards the end of 2000, the Division of Clinical Psychology established a working group to review the accreditation criteria employed by the Committee on Training in Clinical Psychology. The main impetus for this review was the projected rise in numbers of clinical psychology trainees. The National Health Service Executive is aiming for clinical psychology training places in England to increase from 390 in 2000–1 to 546–682 in 2003–4. It is anticipated that there will be parallel increases in Wales, Scotland and Northern Ireland (Gray, 2001). There is general agreement within the profession that current training arrangements are too inflexible to accommodate the increased number of trainees and there is widespread recognition that existing courses might benefit from reconsidering their aims and objectives to reflect changes in the NHS.

The Working Group is still debating possible changes in the accreditation criteria with members of the DCP through a series of consultation papers. The main result of the amendments is likely to be more flexibility in the way individual courses can satisfy the criteria. The Working Group's proposed revisions retain the central features of the existing training schemes: an integrated, generic training; a developmental approach covering the lifespan of potential clients; and the scientist-practitioner model. However, the Group is considering a 'competency-based approach' and has attempted to identify the elements of professional competence in a number of areas: transferable skills; psychological assessment, formulation and intervention; evaluation; research; personal and professional skills (including ethics); communication and teaching; and service delivery. The most contentious aspect of the proposed changes is a move away from the existing requirement of 'core experience' in work with children and adolescents, adults, older adults and people with learning disabilities. The Working Group still recommends that trainees should work with clients across the lifespan, with a wide range of problems and levels of intellectual functioning, but it suggests that the requisite experience may be gained through a variety of training pathways. The revised training arrangements are intended to be more responsive than current provisions to changing patterns of service delivery, nationally determined service priorities and recruitment difficulties in particular specialities/local areas.

While the Working Group continues to canvass opinion about these proposed changes, other alternatives to the existing full-time three-year doctoral programmes are being discussed in different forums. It seems likely that the training role of NHS clinical psychology departments will be expanded (Gray, 2001). At the National Clinical Psychology Conference in Scotland in January 2002, for example, a number of options were discussed. These included a nationally co-ordinated, modular system of training to complement existing university courses. These new flexible training courses would devolve more responsibility for teaching as well as clinical supervision to local NHS departments. Within this model, psychology graduates entering assistant psychologist posts would be able to begin formal training in the modular system, with the option of progressing to the full doctoral qualification over time. Another option discussed at the conference was an alternative to the present model of generic training. It was suggested that 'fast track' (one-year) training of psychology graduates to become single-speciality clinicians (e.g. working with older adults only) would provide a rapid influx of skilled staff in specialities where there are particularly pressing service needs. Within this model, these single-speciality clinicians would be expected to work in their chosen area for a limited time (for example two years), but would then be able to claim advanced standing on a doctoral course if they wished to pursue further training. As noted above, clinical psychology training in Scotland now falls within the remit of SCPMDE, which is itself under the umbrella of the special health board NHS Education for Scotland (NES). This arrangement has only existed for 18 months at the time of writing, so the full implications of these changes remain unclear. However, it is already apparent that there will be greater emphasis under the new arrangements on flexibility of training provisions to meet the growing demand for psychologists with a range of skills.

The concept of an intermediate grade of psychologist between assistant and qualified clinician is not, in fact, new. Burton and Adcock (1998) reported on the establishment of an associate psychologist grade within the Mancunian Community Health (NHS) Trust. This grade was established after consultation with the DCP and the impetus again came from the difficulty in recruiting qualified staff despite the plethora of experienced assistant psychologists within the system. Assistant psychologists with more than two years' experience were invited to apply for re-grading. In this scheme, re-grading is based on assessment of a portfolio produced by the psychologist, demonstrating competency in a range of domains. Candidates are expected to be 'functioning largely independently', with monthly supervision, and working at an 'intellectual and critical level equivalent to university masters level' (Burton and Adcock, 1998: 10). It is anticipated that some of these associate psychologists will eventually apply for clinical psychology training.

Kinderman (2001) outlines yet another alternative to the current training provisions. He suggests we follow the example of the medical profession and restructure existing clinical psychology departments to include permanent intern posts. These posts would be filled by trainees on a rotational basis and trainees would be salaried through the training courses – as they are at present. Kinderman argues that this system would provide significantly more 'supervised placements' than the current system and would strengthen the professional, training and managerial roles of departments. He also addresses the related issue of the career structure in clinical psychology and notes that this needs to be restructured to accommodate graduate psychologists (such as those filling the 1,000 posts in primary care promised by the Department of Health), assistant psychologists, trainee clinical psychologists in their capacity as interns, clinical psychologists and consultant (Grade B) psychologists.

In summary, the path towards the clinical psychology doctorate can be expected to broaden in the very near future to incorporate alternatives to the three-year full-time doctoral programmes. In-service training will probably assume a larger, more formal role, in tandem with the contributions of the university courses, and some form of modular training is likely to emerge. The career structure in clinical psychology is also likely to become more elaborate, incorporating additional grades linked to a revised salary structure. In addition, the introduction of clinical governance in the NHS means that there is going to be an increased emphasis on *post-qualification training* in all professions. In the final section we consider the implications of this development for clinical psychology.

Clinical governance and continuing professional development

Clinical psychology's *Code of Conduct* states:

> Psychologists shall endeavour to maintain and develop their professional competence, to recognize and work within its limits, and to identify and ameliorate factors which restrict it. (BPS, 1998: Section 2:1)

During the last two years, the Division of Clinical Psychology has formalised this requirement, producing *Guidelines for Continuing Professional Development* (CPD; BPS, 2001b). This development is in line with the new emphasis on clinical governance in NHS policy documents. The concept of clinical governance (which is under-pinned by continuing professional development) was introduced in the government White Paper *The New NHS: Modern, Dependable* (DoH, 1997) and developed in *A First Class Service: Quality in the NHS* (DoH, 1998) where it was defined as

a framework through which NHS organisations are accountable for continually improving the quality of their services and safeguarding high standards of care by creating an environment in which excellence in clinical care will flourish.

In a briefing document for the DCP, Hall and Firth-Cozens explain the relationship between clinical governance and CPD:

Clinical governance assumes the existence of a range of skills. Where these do not exist, training will be needed. Training will be required in several different areas, and delivered in a number of different ways. *Lifelong learning* is the term used in the Clinical Governance literature to describe this broad approach to con-tinuing professional development (CPD). The principles underlying CPD should be an integration of legitimate aspirations of individual health professionals, and a response to local service development needs and patient expectations. (Hall and Firth-Cozens, 2000)

As the BPS continues to press the government for statutory regis-tration and regulation of professions 'concerned (wholly or partly) with the physical or mental health of individuals', CPD also under-pins the requirement for chartered psychologists to demonstrate that they are 'maintain(ing) their professional competence to pro-vide the psychological services they are offering or agreeing to provide' (BPS, 2001a: Statute 13).

The DCP *Guidelines for CPD* (2001a) state that full-time clinical psychologists should have a minimum entitlement of ten days a year for CPD activities, including private study, with a pro-rata entitle-ment for part-time staff. Furthermore, psychologists are now required to record these activities in a CPD Log. It is recommended that CPD 'should extend beyond purely clinical applications to include the development of skills and knowledge such as research and development, audit and evaluation, management and organisa-tional issues' (BPS, 2001b: 5). The guidelines also stipulate that clinical psychologists should receive supervision of their work throughout their careers, and should attend an annual professional review with a senior colleague in order to identify their development needs and priorities.

Despite the persuasive and encouraging rhetoric surrounding the renewed emphasis on CPD in the NHS, there are concerns in all professional groups that it will not be adequately resourced and will therefore fail to meet the very real training needs of staff. There must also be a significant change of ethos if CPD in the NHS is to develop according to the principles described above by Hall and Firth-Cozens. One of us (DP) has been involved in discussion of training needs through a local workforce confederation while the other (KC) has been involved in the same debate through a regional initiative to meet the needs of clients with histories of severe childhood trauma, and the staff who work with them. These experiences have highlighted the difficulty of obtaining backing from individual professions and NHS Trusts for interdisciplinary training to address local service needs beyond the level of occasional one-day workshops. However, within clinical psychology, the DCP *Guidelines for CPD* have been welcomed by some in the hope that they will both assist self-regulation within the profession and enable individuals to make a stronger case for study leave and CPD funding with their employers. Certainly, if managed well, a more comprehensive CPD system should enable clinical psychologists to become more responsive to 'local service development needs' by assisting them to acquire new skills for new roles. In the following chapter we will examine the many roles that clinical psychologists occupy within the NHS and other institutions.

Notes

1 The research requirement varies from course to course in terms of the form it takes and when trainees are expected to complete the work, but all the courses include research training and trainees are typically expected to undertake a substantial project during their second and third years.

2 In addition to clinical supervisors and their university-based directors of studies the trainees on the Edinburgh course are encouraged to choose a personal tutor who will not have an evaluative role at any stage and can provide advice and support. Historically, the uptake is low and trainees generally rely on each other for emotional support – a finding also reported in a survey of clinical psychology trainees across Britain (Cushway, 1992).

3 More detailed information about existing clinical psychology training courses may be found in the *Clearing House Handbook* (Appendix). Advice about a career in clinical psychology and training requirements is available on the British Psychological Society website: www.bps.org.uk. An *Alternative Handbook for Training Courses in Clinical Psychology*, providing feedback from previous/existing trainees can also be obtained (Appendix).

4 Approximately 5,500 wte (whole time equivalent) qualified clinical psychologists are employed in the NHS in England, Scotland and Wales.

5 The University of Hertfordshire, Queens' University (Belfast) and University College (Dublin) do not participate in the CHPCCP scheme.

6 The following figures apply to those courses within the Clearing House system.

7 'Chartered Clinical Psychologist' is used to designate individuals who have voluntarily applied to join the BPS Register of Chartered Psychologists, and have been vetted and accepted by the Membership and Qualifications Board. This Register was authorised by the Privy Council in 1987 following the failure of the BPS to obtain government support for legislation to enforce full registration of psychologists.

8 Salaries are about to be renegotiated on a different scale: see Chapter 4.

9 At present assistant psychologists are typically paid £12,978–£14,598 while trainee salaries begin at £15,185; these scales will be revised when salaries of qualified staff are renegotiated (see Chapter 4, p. 65).

4

CAREERS IN CLINICAL PSYCHOLOGY

In this chapter we will describe the different applications of clinical psychology and the diverse settings in which clinical psychologists work. A number of our colleagues have contributed to this chapter, to enable us to provide accounts of clinical specialities written by individuals working in those fields. We will also consider the many roles that members of the profession occupy in addition to their clinical role, including those of clinical supervisor, teacher/trainer, researcher, consultant, and manager.

We will begin by providing an overview of the roles available to clinical psychologists, before proceeding to describe the different fields of clinical work in more detail.

What do we do and where do we work?

One of the undoubted attractions of clinical psychology is that entry into the profession opens doors leading in numerous directions. The generic training equips graduates to work with individuals of all ages, with a wide range of physical and mental health problems. One not only has a choice at the outset, but it is also relatively easy to change direction as one's career progresses. In Britain, the NHS employs the vast majority of clinical psychologists, while the remainder work in academic, social work or forensic settings. Clinical psychologists in academic posts also generally spend part of their time working in the NHS, pursuing clinical and research interests. To date, very few clinical psychologists have moved into full-time private practice in this country, although an increasing number do a limited amount of private work in addition to their NHS work, providing both therapy and opinions on cases under litigation.

Within the NHS, many clinical psychologists combine work in different areas through split posts. Given the current shortage of qualified staff, it is still relatively easy to pick up some sessions in one's chosen clinical field even if a full-time job is not available. Split posts can be arranged in a variety of ways. One might work with one client group (for example, adults with severe and enduring mental health problems) in different settings, perhaps spending part of the week in a day hospital and the rest of one's time in outpatient clinics. Split posts combining different specialities are also common: for example, working part-time with adults with learning disabilities and working part-time with children. Newly qualified staff often prefer split posts because they provide an opportunity to investigate different areas of work more thoroughly before deciding where one's real interest lies. However, experienced clinicians may also opt for split posts, perhaps feeling that the diversity helps to keep them interested and motivated.

At the time of writing, the grading and salary structure within clinical psychology is about to be reviewed as part of the government's Agenda for Change strategy that will evaluate the jobs of all NHS staff besides doctors, dentists and senior managers and then map these evaluated posts on to new pay scales (Department of Health, 2002). A review of the grading and salary structure in clinical psychology is certainly overdue. Qualified clinical psychologists currently progress through A Grade (salary £17,078–£38,919) before seeking promotion to B Grade/Consultant posts (salary £37,421–£62,312). Mirroring the situation in medicine, there has been a shortage of B Grade posts in some areas and specialities, leading to frustration among experienced psychologists looking for promotion. While the details of the Agenda for Change re-gradings are still being worked out, the DCP is cautiously welcoming the proposed review and is lobbying the Department of Health for comparable pay for consultant clinical psychologists, doctors, dentists and senior management. The DCP is also keen to ensure that there is agreement on suitable criteria for career and pay progression and that newly qualified psychologists enter the pay structure at an appropriately high level.

Where do we work?

Clinical psychologists work in lots of different settings. There is a growing trend towards location of services in primary care, and we will consider this in more detail in Chapter 5. At present, adult (18–65 years) psychological services are most developed in primary care, although initiatives to develop primary-care-based psychological services for children and older adults are also under way in some places. Psychologists based in primary care work quite autonomously, with varying degrees of integration into the primary care teams.

Some psychologists who are based in the community do not work in NHS premises. They may deliver services to a particular client group (for example, individuals who are misusing drugs and/or alcohol; children who have been abused; women who have experienced domestic violence) through an agency funded by the social services or, less commonly, the voluntary sector. Clinical psychologists also see people in their own home or place of residence.

Despite the growth of community and primary-care-based services, many clinical psychologists still work in psychiatric hospitals or the psychiatric wards/units of general hospitals. Some of these clinicians will see people referred by their GPs in hospital-based outpatient clinics, but clinical psychologists also work with clients with more acute, or severe and enduring difficulties, who may be inpatients or day patients. These clients usually require a multidisciplinary team approach, and the psychologists will liaise closely with nurses, psychiatrists, occupational therapists and other workers to provide appropriate input for each individual. Clients seen in these settings include children, adolescents, adults, older adults, and people with learning disabilities who also have mental health problems.

Clinical psychologists also work with other client groups in general hospitals or specialist centres. Some psychologists work with clients with physical health problems when psychological factors are contributing to their difficulties. Oncology, diabetic, cardiac and pain clinics/units are examples of services that frequently request clinical psychology input. Clinical neuropsychologists specialise in the assessment and management of acquired brain injury, and may work in hospitals or community settings.

While the majority of clinical work consists of assessing clients' needs and delivering treatment, service development is also an important part of many jobs. This can range from offering a new therapy programme within an existing service (for example, starting a therapy group for people with binge-eating disorders attending an outpatient centre) to starting an entirely new service, such as a primary care clinic for children with sleep disorders.

How is treatment delivered?

Most clinical work consists of *one-to-one* assessment and therapy/treatment. Individual work may also benefit from the involvement of the client's partner/significant other. This input can provide the therapist with additional information about the client's difficulties, as well as giving the therapist an opportunity to inform the significant other about how he/she might better support the client (see, for example, Gold, 2000). *Group therapy* may be offered when there are sufficient numbers of clients with similar problems, and is particularly appropriate in day hospitals and inpatient units. *Couple therapy* is used when relationship difficulties are central to the presenting problem, while psychologists working with children and adolescents frequently employ *family therapy,* involving all family members, or at least those most closely involved with the client. Clinical psychologists also work indirectly with clients as *consultants,* by providing advice for carers or other professionals about how to assist the client to overcome his/her difficulties.

What do clinical psychologists do besides clinical work?

In addition to their clinical commitments, clinical psychologists are regularly involved in *teaching/training* and *supervision* of colleagues. The clinical psychology doctoral courses rely heavily on teaching input from NHS psychologists in addition to the teaching provided by staff in academic posts. Clinical psychologists are also frequently expected to offer training for other health professionals, particularly nursing staff, and care staff in non-NHS facilities, such as residential settings for adults with learning disabilities that are run by the social work department. More informally, clinical psychologists routinely provide support and advice to other staff regarding psychological aspects of their work.

Sometimes clinical psychologists are asked to supervise non-psychologists, while supervision of both clinical psychology trainees and colleagues is a routine part of the job for all members of the profession since the DCP stipulates that all clinical psychologists should receive regular casework supervision.

In keeping with the scientist-practitioner model, *research* is identified as a core skill of its members in the DCP's statement of the *Core Purpose and Philosophy of the Profession* (DCP, 2001b). NHS psychologists have historically been less productive than their academic colleagues in terms of research activity, if this productivity is measured by numbers of publications in peer-reviewed journals (see Chapter 2, p. 38). This disparity is usually explained as the inevitable consequence of the heavy clinical workloads of NHS clinicians in all disciplines, including psychology. However, it is arguably both increasingly important for NHS clinical psychologists to become involved in research, and increasingly feasible for them to do so. There is a strong trend towards evidence-based practice in medicine and psychology, and part of this trend is a growing emphasis on *effectiveness.* While the large, randomised controlled trials (RCTs) that have traditionally been viewed as the gold standard in clinical research measured *efficacy* (what worked under rigorously controlled conditions), clinicians and health economists are becoming more aware of the importance of investigating what is *effective*: what works in the real world when less carefully selected (i.e. more representative) clients are treated by clinicians with the skills one would typically find outside a specialist centre. There is a pressing need for clinical research in community/primary care centres in the UK, since most of the evidence base we have for psychological interventions comes from trials conducted in hospital populations, or specialist centres, with the majority of research findings coming from the USA. The methodology required for investigating effective practice is more manageable for busy clinicians than that required by large RCTs, and it is essential that future research reflects the priorities of those delivering the care to service users in this country.

A further role occupied by many senior clinical psychologists is a *managerial* one. Most commonly this entails management of other psychologists within a clinical psychology department. Increasingly, clinical psychology departments are also recruiting staff with other professional backgrounds – such as nurse therapists, counselling psychologists and health psychologists – which generates other challenges for managers (Paxton, 2000). Managerial responsibilities may be assumed by clinical psychologists beyond their own departments: for example in multidisciplinary teams that include psychiatrists, psychologists, nurses, occupational therapists, social workers and others. A small number of clinical psychologists have also taken on managerial roles at NHS Trust level as clinical directors.

Now that we have considered the role of the clinical psychologist in broad terms, we will examine it in more detail by describing the main client groups with whom we work.

The client groups

Children and young people

The last few years have seen an expansion in the provision of psychological services to children and young people, with the recognition of the impact that intervention can make in the treatment and prevention of psychological problems. Clinical psychologists who specialise in working with children and families provide a range of services in a variety of settings. They are trained in assessment, formulation and treatment of numerous difficulties and provide both teaching and consultancy to other professionals, such as health visitors and social workers. Many psychologists are also engaged in service development and evaluation.

Clinical child psychologists draw upon a broad theoretical base in the formulation of problems and application of psychological therapies. They typically accept referrals of children and young people from 0–18 years, which adds an important developmental dimension to the work. Clinical child psychologists seek to develop collaborative partnerships with children and their parents in order to promote psychological well-being and the resolution of their difficulties. This may be direct work with children and young people, work with parents to develop and enhance parent–child relationships, or provision of group therapies for children or parents. Psychological interventions may also be facilitated by supporting and supervising other professionals, promoting the wider use of psychological approaches (Carr, 1999).

Psychologists also contribute to various specialist types of multidisciplinary team, such as paediatric liaison teams, child development teams and youth offending teams, as well as child and adolescent mental health services and to services providing inpatient acute care or input for more complex and enduring mental health problems. The demand for services is often very high (BPS, 2001c).

The problems that clinical child psychologists are likely to encounter vary significantly, depending upon the setting in which they are delivering a service and the type of work they are doing. Common psychological problems typically present as parenting and behavioural problems, such as temper tantrums, problems of aggression and over-activity, enuresis/soiling, feeding and sleeping problems. Psychologists also work with children who have emotional and relationship difficulties, including anxiety and depression, phobias, obsessive-compulsive disorder, post-traumatic stress and psychosomatic conditions. Children at most risk of developing psychological problems often live in areas of socioeconomic disadvantage. Others at high risk include looked-after children, children who have been physically, sexually or emotionally abused, children suffering from problems of communication or learning and those coping with chronic illness where compliance with medication is important (Meltzer et al., 2000; BPS, 2001c). Other presenting problems relate to family issues such as divorce/separation or bereavement, and those likely to arise in adolescence such as eating disorders, drug abuse and conduct disorders.

There is recognition that psychological problems that begin in childhood tend to persist into adulthood if they are not adequately treated and have significant implications for psychological well-being and development across the lifespan. This can sometimes lead to transmission and perpetuation of problems in subsequent generations by particular family interaction patterns (Dadds, 1995). A recent survey reported that approximately one in ten children from a population of 10,000 had mental health problems that were significant enough to impact upon day-to-day life (Meltzer et al., 2000). This highlights the need for further development and provision of psychological care. The importance of early intervention and prevention is increasingly being recognised and psychologists are beginning to play a role in this kind of work, such as helping mothers suffering from post-natal depression, and developing early parenting programmes.

S. Hughes

Adults with mental health problems

The majority of clinical work takes place with adults (18–65 years), and the range of presenting problems is vast. In primary care clinical psychologists may work alongside counsellors employed by the NHS, or may refer clients on to counsellors working in non-statutory agencies. Counsellors typically see people with less complex problems who do not require structured psychological therapy but are likely to benefit from an opportunity to ventilate their distress, clarify the problems facing them, engage in appropriate problem-solving and identify more effective coping strategies. Most of the referrals to clinical psychology departments come from GPs, and many of the clients they refer are suffering from depression and/or an anxiety disorder, such as generalised anxiety, agoraphobia, panic disorder, social anxiety, obsessive-compulsive disorder or post-traumatic stress disorder. Individuals may also be referred with eating disorders, problematic alcohol/drug use, unresolved grief reactions or complex interpersonal difficulties. Many clients present with more than one area of difficulty, and some problems have been present for a number of years before professional help is sought. Mental health professionals, including psychologists, are becoming more aware of how many clients have a history of abuse or neglect. Some of these individuals bear very deep psychological (and sometimes physical) scars, and may need long-term therapy in order to achieve an acceptable quality of life.

Clinical psychologists who have been in the profession a long time comment on the increase in the severity of the problems referred over the years. In theory, more severe long-term difficulties should be dealt with in secondary care, but many clinical psychologists working in primary care find themselves in situations where secondary services are not available for clients they would otherwise refer to such services. This inevitably places stress on the primary care team. The group most likely to slip through the net of the secondary services are the individuals traditionally labelled as suffering from personality disorders, many of whom are now recognised to be displaying the effects of severe childhood abuse/neglect. Since these individuals are frequently high users of services (many have a history of self-harm and tend to go from crisis to crisis), they pose a substantial challenge to primary care teams (including the psychologists working with these teams) where there are no adequate secondary/tertiary or non-statutory services to meet their particular needs.

Most severe and enduring mental health problems are, however, dealt with by secondary or tertiary services. Individuals diagnosed as suffering from schizophrenia or bi-polar disorder form the majority of this group. Clinical psychologists working with these clients (a speciality often described as psychiatric rehabilitation) are likely to see them in a range of settings: in day hospitals, as outpatients, and at home. Although most of these clients experience repeated hospital admissions, provision of psychological services is generally inadequate on the wards. A recent study of 38 acute psychiatric wards found that only 11 per cent of inpatients had had any contact with a psychologist (Sainsbury Centre, 1997–8).

Therapeutic work with individuals who have severe and enduring mental health problems usually involves extensive liaison with other professionals. Many of these clients are on complex medication regimes for treatment of their psychoses and these will be established and reviewed by a psychiatrist. In addition, community psychiatric nurses, occupational therapists and social workers are often involved to assist with the range of difficulties associated with long-term mental health problems. These difficulties include unemployment, unsuitable housing, financial problems, relationship breakdowns and lack/loss of basic life skills, such as the confidence to go out and the ability to manage a budget.

Goodwin (2001) discusses the challenges that face clinical psychologists working in psychiatric rehabilitation and suggests that psychologists are likely to find it frustrating if they define their task as the provision of psychological therapy to referred clients on an outpatient basis. She encourages psychologists to take a more systemic view and conceive of their role as 'supporting the overall service system to do the best it can for clients', which will involve supporting other staff in the system as well as spending dedicated time with clients.

A recent development in the provision of services for adults with severe and enduring mental health problems has been the formation of Assertive Outreach programmes. The model was developed in the United States in the context of under-developed community mental health care and was included in the *National Service Framework for Mental Health* (Department of Health, 1999a), with the expectation that Assertive Outreach would be operating in Britain by April 2002. The model calls for user involvement in shaping the service, which aims to be accessible 24 hours a day, deliver care in clients' own communities, and provide support on an indefinite basis. The service is delivered through a number of channels: dedicated teams; individual outreach workers; and extended remits of existing rehabilitation/community mental health teams. Outcome studies from the USA and Australia suggest that Assertive Outreach can reduce hospital admissions and produce an improvement in clients' health and quality of life, but the model has still to be evaluated here (Meddings, 1999; Meddings and Cupitt, 2000; Cupitt, 2001).

K. Cheshire

Older adults

Clinical psychology services for older people (those aged over 65 years) are largely specialist secondary, or in some cases, tertiary care services. Many developed within psychiatric services and often make a distinction between older people with organic problems (primarily dementia) and 'functional' problems (e.g. anxiety or depression). Clinical psychologists work with both groups of patients in a range of services – day hospitals, in-patient facilities (both hospital and community-based) and as part of community mental health teams. Referrals to these teams come primarily from psychiatrists but also from GPs and social services. Psychologists also work with voluntary and community groups, e.g. Help the Aged. Some services see people younger than 65 if their problems are similar to those more usually associated with old age, such as early onset dementia. Clinical psychologists also work within medical services for older people. Some such provision is very specific, e.g. into stroke rehabilitation services, but other provision is more general, e.g. into in-patient medical facilities. Recent years have seen services for older people beginning to develop in primary care (BPS, 2002a). The majority of older people do not have psychological problems. However, those that do experience the same range of problems as younger people. Anxiety-related problems are common (Watts et al., 2002) and can contribute to other problems such as failure to recover from a fall. If not treated, anxiety can lead to severe reductions in an older person's functioning and leave him/her more at risk of physical health problems. Depression is less common but has been identified as the most significant health problem in later life (Copeland et al., 1992). For a minority, bereavement leaves them vulnerable to depression and increased mortality and suicide risk. Up to 6 per cent of people aged 65 years and over are affected by dementia (e.g. Alzheimer's disease), with as many as 20 per cent of people aged 85 and over affected (Mann et al., 1992; Copeland et al., 1992). Challenging behaviour can be precipitated by organic conditions and by emotional reactions to loss or relocation, e.g. following a move to residential care.

Many older people with physical health problems do not consider their difficulties to be a major handicap (Leonard and Burns, 2000). However, a disproportionate number do suffer from psychological complications, e.g. following a fall or the development of a respiratory disorder or stroke (Kiseley and Goldberg, 1996).

The work of clinical psychologists in services for older people is underpinned by the same principles as the work of psychologists in other areas and there are many similarities in what they do. Direct clinical work employs individual, group and family approaches. Indirect work includes training and consultancy with staff and carers in a range of settings. However, there are some distinctive features of the work in services for older people (BPS, 2002a). These include: a knowledge base in gerontology; adapting therapy to better match the emphases of later life development (such as preparation for death); a greater need for anticipatory socialisation to a psychological approach; the existence of more iatrogenic complaints; the need for neuropsychological assessment in relation to organically based cognitive impairment; and an emphasis on counteracting ageism in systems. There is also the obvious need for knowledge of age-related settings and liaison with age-specialised colleagues and organisations. The *National Service Framework for Older People* (Department of Health, 2001c) has implications for the work of clinical psychologists, at least in England and Wales (Boddington, 2001; Lee et al., 2002).

The development of specialist services can be seen as an assertive response to ageism and exclusion – ring-fenced services mean that older people's needs do not get pushed aside. However, a paradoxical effect of 'positive compensation' can be to exclude a group from equality of access to good quality mainstream health services. Many older people who could benefit from psychological help are not referred to secondary-care-based services. The few places where primary care services have developed illustrate their efficacy in ameliorating distress and preventing deterioration in psychological and physical health (McGarry et al.,1997; Baty, 1998; Fothergill, 2000). The primary care focus of the 'new' NHS provides both opportunity and challenge for clinical psychologists. Does a specialist service offer the best way of ensuring that the needs of older people are met? Would a combined generic/specialist service – linking with primary care services for younger people – be more effective? The responses to such questions will be the key to the future development of clinical psychology services for older people (BPS, 2002a).

F. Baty

People with intellectual disabilities

People with intellectual disabilities (also referred to as learning disability in the UK) are referred to clinical psychologists with the same type and range of problems found in people without intellectual disabilities. One major difference is that the majority of referrals of these individuals (currently at least) come from sources other than GPs. Very few individuals with an intellectual disability refer themselves to clinical psychology and most referrals come from a carer, social worker or day centre staff member. In the case of children and young people referrals may come from a paediatrician, teacher or other professionals in child health and education. A further difference is that the 'reason' for the referral may often be described as a behaviour problem rather than as a clinical condition such as anxiety or depression. One possible reason for this is that individuals with intellectual disability may have difficulty in understanding and communicating their feelings and thoughts, so behavioural problems may mask underlying difficulties or changes in mood and anxiety. Such individuals are more vulnerable than the general population to the development of severe mental health problems, and also may have more (sometimes undiagnosed) physical health problems. Both mental and physical health problems can give rise to behavioural disturbance because of communication difficulties. The role of the clinical psychologist is to carefully assess the nature of an individual's problem(s) and decide how they might be solved or alleviated by applying psychological principles.

Where psychological treatment is appropriate many clinical psychologists in intellectual disability work within a broadly behavioural framework, but the use of psychodynamic, cognitive-behavioural, and systemic approaches is also rapidly developing.

Very often the problem that needs to be solved does not belong solely to the person with the intellectual disability, but may also belong to the carers or staff working with that individual. As a result much work is indirect, and involves consultancy with and training of carers and other individuals working with service users. One of the challenges for clinical psychology in this area is that it often requires multi-agency work and involvement in more than one domain of a service user's life, e.g. education, accommodation, day services and employment. This may be particularly salient during times of transition.

Clinical psychologists who work with people with intellectual disabilities usually work in multidisciplinary community teams that may include social workers as well as other health care professionals such as psychiatrists, community nurses, speech and language therapists, occupational therapists, physiotherapists, pharmacists, dieticians and podiatrists. Some clinical psychologists only work with either children or adults; others work with individuals across the lifespan.

Although many clinical psychologists in intellectual disability work generically, a number of specialisms are now developing, focused on service users with similar levels of need. Opportunities now exist for clinical psychologists to specialise in work with service users who present with challenging behaviour; dual diagnosis, i.e. intellectual disability and severe mental health problems; service users with forensic needs and service users who have developmental disorders, such as autistic spectrum disorder. Whether working generically or in a specialism, clinical psychologists may develop their own interests, which might be an interest in particular types of assessment or treatment approach.

A number of intellectual disability psychology departments also have active research interests, which contribute to the development of good practice and quality service provision. One consequence is that these departments often employ graduate psychologists who are interested in training in clinical psychology as assistant psychologists.

Over the last four or five decades there have been many changes in social policy in the field of intellectual disability; one significant change has been the gradual closure of long-stay hospitals, which have been replaced by community-based residential and day service provision. As well as being affected by changes in social policy, clinical psychologists have positively influenced some of the changes that have taken place, particularly the development of person-centred and holistic ways of working. They have also been active in supporting the concept of inclusion, i.e. helping individuals with learning disabilities develop roles and access services which are available to everyone in society. One of the challenges for clinical psychologists working in intellectual disability in the future is to support inclusive practice, while at the same time providing a service which sensitively supports and meets the specialist health needs of people with an intellectual disability.

B. Walley

Clinical psychology in physical health care

This speciality has developed as health care has moved away from the traditional biomedical approach to one which recognises the importance of psychosocial factors in health and disease. The US Surgeon-General has reported that 50 per cent of the causes of premature death and disability are due to 'behavioural and lifestyle' factors, many of which are psychological in origin. Research has shown that up to 75 per cent of all GP consultations are psychological in nature (Saxby and Svanberg, 1998).

Clinical psychologists in physical health care may be involved in health promotion, the direct and indirect care of patients, consultancy to other health professionals and research. The two main specialist areas within the NHS are physical rehabilitation and health psychology.

PHYSICAL REHABILITATION SERVICES   The majority of specialist physical rehabilitation services are provided by multidisciplinary teams in both inpatient and community settings. Most rehabilitation services see patients within the age-range 18–65 years; outside this range the paediatric or older adult services are utilised. The physical rehabilitation services mainly see patients with both traumatic and non-traumatic brain injury; multiple sclerosis; motor neurone disease and other neurological disorders; and rheumatic diseases. Ideally (and usually) the patient is transferred to a specialist inpatient rehabilitation unit immediately after the acute phase of the illness/injury has passed. At this stage a comprehensive multidisciplinary assessment is carried out by the team, which consists of psychological, medical and nursing specialists and the relevant professions allied to medicine (PAMs).

The aim and emphasis of a clinical psychology service in physical rehabilitation is:

- assessment and advice regarding the management of neuro-psychological deficits;
- assessment and intervention to address the emotional and psychological sequelae of physical disability at all levels as appropriate;
- restoration of function following a traumatic event, e.g. brain injury;
- care aims of preventing deterioration and/or relapse, e.g. arthritis;
- management of deterioration in progressive disease, e.g. multiple sclerosis, motor neurone disease;
- education and support for families and carers.

In many services there are designated inpatient facilities which provide a range of essential physical therapies as well as specialist medical, nursing and psychological care. The in-patient setting is mostly utilised for assessment, prevention of deterioration and restoration of function. The majority of the remaining work is usually provided in community settings (e.g. local health centres or the person's own home) in order to monitor individuals following discharge and to maintain patients with progressive disorders.

Clinical psychologists working in physical rehabilitation may offer a range of approaches, such as one-to-one therapy; specific interventions for couples, e.g. psychosexual counselling; group interventions, e.g. multiple sclerosis management and support groups; and consultancy to carers (professional and family). The specialist knowledge and skills of the clinical psychologist are of prime importance, given the neurological and cognitive sequelae experienced by the majority of patients requiring the service. As such, clinical psychologists in physical rehabilitation usually undertake further qualification in neuropsychology as well as continuing professional development in specific areas such as rheumatology and neurological disorders.

HEALTH PSYCHOLOGY   Health psychology is a recognised subdivision of the BPS with defined aims and objectives:

- To study scientifically the psychological processes of health, illness and healthcare
- To apply psychology to :

  (a) the promotion and maintenance of health
  (b) the analysis and improvement of the health care system and health policy formation
  (c) the prevention of illness and disability and the enhancement of outcomes of those who are ill or disabled

- To develop professional skills in research, consultancy and teaching/training

(Health Psychology AGM, 2000)

The Division of Health Psychology has developed core competencies for professional qualification in health psychology that may be achieved by clinical psychologists through further academic study and research, together with relevant practical experience.

The majority of patients referred to health psychologists for psychological assessment and support are experiencing chronic and/or life-threatening diseases. The age range is 18 years and upwards and since many diseases are degenerative in origin, there tends to be no upper age limit. Referrals mainly come from hospital consultants in, for example, cardiology and respiratory medicine, oncology, palliative care, chronic pain, gynaecology, obstetrics, general medical and surgical specialities. A smaller number of patients are referred by GPs. Health psychologists become involved with these patients

- when the person experiences persistent psychological distress beyond 'normal' levels, e.g. clinical anxiety and depression;
- to aid coping with/amelioration of symptoms, e.g. pain and/or treatment side-effects such as anticipatory nausea and vomiting;
- to help individuals to manage difficulty in compliance with treatment;
- to support patients and families in making complex treatment decisions;
- to undertake cognitive assessment, e.g. suspected brain dysfunction which may affect decision-making and/or coping processes

Psychologists working in this field offer systematic, comprehensive, psychological assessment and provide appropriate treatment interventions. A range of therapeutic interventions may be utilised depending upon the individual therapist's specific skills including, for example, cognitive-behavioural, psychodynamic and interpersonal therapy approaches.

Interventions may be offered on a one-to-one basis, to couples, or in a group setting, and require a flexible and adaptable approach to working. A systemic approach involving consultancy to other professionals in the psychosocial aspects of healthcare (indirect care) is a regular feature of health psychology input. Clinical psychologists are also becoming more involved in service planning and development.

Other areas of input may be in primary and secondary prevention: for example, in coronary artery disease and hypertension. Behavioural methods, counselling and cognitive approaches to behaviour change have been found to reduce risk in a number of studies (Patel et al., 1985; Lewin et al., 1992).

The clinical psychologist may work as part of a multidisciplinary team (e.g. in a breast care clinic) or may receive individual referrals. Whilst many patients are seen at their acute NHS Trust, both as inpatients and outpatients, a significant number are seen in local health centres, community hospitals, hospices and in their own homes, depending upon need.

Due to the recognition of the importance of the role of psychosocial factors in illness and disease, clinical psychology can offer an important perspective on health at the individual and societal levels. Psychological theories and principles can help both service and policy development to better address the health needs of the population.

K. McGarva

Adults with substance misuse problems

Excessive use of alcohol, nicotine and other drugs can lead to a range of health, psychological and social problems. Cancer, heart disease, major infections, dependence, cognitive impairment, depression, suicide, family breakdown, job loss, criminal behaviour and homelessness are just some of the more serious risks. Health statistics indicate that the number of individuals in the UK experiencing problems related to substance misuse is vast. It is of particular concern that a growing number of children and adolescents are developing such problems (Department of Health, 1999b).

Substance misuse services in the UK are relatively thin on the ground compared to the size of the problem. The only professional help that many people are likely to access will be from their GP. Specialist help is typically provided on a regional basis by a multidisciplinary team comprising psychiatrists, psychiatric nurses, psychologists and social workers. Traditionally such teams operated at the secondary care level with a central, dedicated unit offering inpatient, day-patient and outpatient services. Recently these services have tended to extend their work into community settings, such as health centres, and function in a more integrated way with primary care and community-based agencies. Outreach provision has grown to take services to those who, for a variety of reasons, normally might not access them. In most areas there are specialist non-statutory agencies too.

The number of clinical psychology posts in substance misuse in the UK is small compared to other specialities such as adult mental health or child and family services. However, there has been growth in drug misuse service posts since the late 1980s, largely as a response to the emergence of HIV infection. Most clinical psychology posts in substance misuse exist within a multidisciplinary team. This reflects the multiple needs of substance misusers. However, some departments are organised such that individual clinical psychologists working in adult mental health and primary care provide assessment and/or treatment in relative isolation to patients with specific substance misuse problems – such as psychologists who run groups in GP practices to help patients stop smoking.

The work of a clinical psychologist in this field can be varied. The psychologist will offer assessment and treatment to help patients change their substance misuse behaviour. Depending on the severity of the misuse and a patient's wishes and resources, the goals of treatment can vary from abstinence to controlled use or harm reduction (for example, continuing to use drugs but not by injection). Treatment may be offered on an individual, group or couple/family basis. Approaches might include client-centred counselling, behavioural methods, problem-solving and cognitive-behaviour therapy. Psychologists have been prominent in developing specific treatment approaches which address explicitly the fact that many substance misusers are ambivalent about change. The transtheoretical model of change (Prochaska et al., 1992) assumes that change is a series of linked processes comprising quite distinct stages (e.g. contemplating a change vs. acting on an intention to change). Therapeutic tasks that are important at one stage might be inappropriate at another. Treatment success will depend on an accurate assessment of which stage the patient has reached. The stage of relapse is built into this model since substance misusers often relapse repeatedly before achieving a more durable period of stability in their behaviour. As a result, treatment can be lengthy. Motivational interviewing (Miller and Rollnick, 1991) is an innovative set of techniques to help patients gain insight into the pros and cons of change and establish commitment to the intention to change.

In addition to treatment targeting the substance misuse, the clinical psychologist may offer treatment for coexisting problems, such as depression, which can be the result, or a significant factor in the development, of the misuse. Clinical psychologists are sometimes also asked to perform neuropsychological assessments because heavy substance misuse, especially involving alcohol or benzodiazepines, can cause permanent cognitive impairments. This information can help in tailoring individual treatment programmes. Finally, as in other specialities, clinical psychologists are well placed by virtue of their training to perform research, including audit and evaluation projects, within the substance misuse field.

Due to the small numbers of clinical psychologists working in substance misuse relative to demand, some advocate that to optimise cost-effectiveness their primary role should be to offer training, supervision and consultancy in psychological approaches to other staff groups rather than direct clinical work with patients. Such system-level service models are increasingly prevalent.

A. Peters

Clinical neuropsychology

Clinical neuropsychologists work in a number of settings with a variety of client groups covering a wide age range. Most of their clients have an established neurological condition, with traumatic brain injury, stroke and dementia being the most common. Clinical neuropsychologists are also quite frequently involved in issues of differential diagnosis (for example, distinguishing depression and dementia). They generally work in a secondary or tertiary level service in acute hospitals, specialist rehabilitation facilities or as part of a community rehabilitation team.

Psychologists working in this field have particular expertise in administering and interpreting neuropsychological assessments. In doing so they are generally interested in trying to tap into underlying brain function and its relation to behaviour rather than measuring an abstract concept such as IQ. This means that the clinical interview and the qualitative aspects of testing are often of greater importance than the numbers that testing yields. Neuropsychologists will typically be interested in a range of cognitive functions including perception, memory and learning, attention, language and visuo-spatial skills. They are especially interested in executive functions: that is, those skills that allow us to plan, problem-solve and engage in flexible goal-directed behaviour. These are important functions that are associated with long-term outcome following brain damage but are frequently missed by traditional tests of intelligence. The neuropsychologist will also wish to assess the emotional impact of the event, as anxiety, depression and personality change are often reported after neurological events. The detailed data obtained through such an assessment can be useful for diagnosis and provides fine-grained information about how an established neurological event has affected behaviour; this information is then used to direct rehabilitation and evaluate treatment.

Clinical neuropsychologists develop rehabilitation programmes for their clients that may be delivered individually or in groups. Some of this rehabilitation may involve cognitive remediation with the aim of restoring previously affected functions, but this has limited proven efficacy and generalisation problems are common. Time is spent assisting clients to develop new skills and employ compensatory strategies that ameliorate their cognitive deficits, e.g. learning to use memory aids. Many clinical neuropsychologists provide individual therapy for depression, anxiety-related disorders and anger problems, all of which are common after neurological insults. They may provide input to the family as well as the individual. In addition, they may advise on environmental manipulation and may work indirectly with clients through relatives or carers.

Until very recently, clinical neuropsychologists have tended to be clinical psychologists with an interest in neuropsychology. Many would have completed a neuropsychology placement as part of their training and/or been engaged in research relevant to clinical neuropsychology, and then developed greater expertise post qualification on a fairly *ad hoc* basis. This position is currently in the process of changing, with the Division of Neuropsychology aiming to develop and accredit post-qualification training courses in clinical neuropsychology.

A. Harper

Clinical psychology in forensic settings

Clinical psychologists who work in forensic settings differ from colleagues working in adult mental health in a number of ways. First, their caseloads tend to be smaller. Second, forensic work is much more orientated towards considerations of risk to others. Third, whilst therapeutic work is still involved it is hedged around by third party interests and the recurrent need to liaise with other agencies such as the Home Office, the police and probation services. There are no fixed ways of working in forensic settings, but consultancy (for other staff), risk assessment and specialist therapy work with high risk clients tend to characterise the field.

Forensic work occurs predominantly within the system of maximum security hospitals (Broadmoor, Ashworth and Rampton in England and Carstairs in Scotland). There are no maximum security facilities in Wales and Northern Ireland. Forensic clinical psychologists are also employed in regional secure units which are less secure than the above (but still virtually impossible to escape from). These are dotted throughout the NHS. For example, in the north-west of England there are three medium secure units. The levels of security reflect risk to public safety as the residents of these facilities are overwhelmingly mentally disordered offenders who were sent to hospital by the courts. Given the high rates of poor mental health in offender populations, offenders who are designated as mentally disordered and sent to hospital rather than prison generally have committed very serious crimes such as rape, homicide or arson. These 'index offences' are the dominant considerations in the referral route to secure mental health settings, not the type or adjudged severity of mental health problem or learning disability. Secure services contain a mixture of psychotic patients, those with learning disabilities and those with a diagnosis of personality disorder. Some are classified as having more than one diagnosis ('dual diagnosis' or 'co-morbidity').

A controversial aspect of forensic work is its social control function – it involves recurrent consideration of public safety and lawfully delegated powers of preventative detention. This has come to the fore recently in discussions about the preventative detention of people with severe and dangerous personality disorder. The British government wants to use new powers under a revised Mental Health Act to detain such people (Department of Health and Home Office, 2000). Most would have committed serious offences but this condition of proven criminality is not stipulated as necessary. The British Psychological Society is currently arguing that any question of dangerousness and the preventative detention of dangerous people should be a criminal justice not health legislation matter. Clinical psychologists currently have no formal powers of detention under mental health legislation. This is likely to change with the new Act, but this will mainly involve forensic clinical psychologists being responsible for those with a diagnosis of personality disorder. We will discuss the implications of these anticipated changes in Chapter 5.

D. Pilgrim

The preceding sections provide some insights into the work currently undertaken by clinical psychologists across a range of settings. More detailed accounts of these roles can be found in texts listed in the Further Reading section at the end of the book. The diversity of roles both enriches and fragments the profession – a point we will return to in Chapter 7. In the following chapter we will consider some of the ways in which the clinical psychologist's role is likely to develop in the near future.

5

CHANGING PRACTICE AND CHANGING ROLES

In the previous chapter we outlined some of the roles that are currently available to clinical psychologists in Britain and noted recent developments in these clinical areas. In this chapter we will look more broadly at the emerging trends in clinical psychology and suggest ways in which our roles and practice may be expected to change in the near future. We will begin by considering how the scientist-practitioner model, the guiding principle of the profession since its inception, is evolving into that of the evidence-based practitioner. We will then discuss how the way in which many of us work is likely to change in response to three specific trends: (1) the growing trend to locate clinical psychology services within primary care in Britain, which has led to further separation between clinical psychology and psychiatry; (2) the increasing emphasis on user involvement in shaping health services, which is likely to drive the further development of community psychology; and (3) the implications of proposed reforms to the Mental Health Act for additional changes in the clinical psychologist's role.

The evidence-based practitioner

In the current political and economic climate, clinical psychology, like the other health professions, is under greater pressure than ever before to demonstrate its effectiveness. The implementation of clinical governance (Department of Health, 1998), research and development initiatives and quality assurance measures in the NHS signals the arrival of protocol and evidence-based practice (EBP). Lawton and Parker (1999) identify three reasons why clinical protocols are being promoted: risk management; facilitation of more rapid implementation of research findings; and standardisation of practice to produce more cost-effective and efficient health care. This trend towards growing proceduralisation of health care is not confined to the NHS, but reflects the *Zeitgeist* in other Western countries. In the USA, private health care providers are increasingly demanding evidence-based practice guidelines and these determine which treatment packages they will cover. The American Psychological Association has recently published the findings of its task force, created to investigate 'empirically supported treatments' for a range of psychological disorders (Dobson and Craig, 1998).

Within clinical psychology, the issue of clinical protocols has so far received less attention than that of EBP, and the response to EBP has been mixed. Certainly, it has aroused considerable debate, and a recent issue of *Clinical Psychology Forum* (November 1999) was devoted to the subject. In the editorial prefacing this issue, Derek Milne argues that the scientist-practitioner model is not interchangeable with that of the evidence-based practitioner. He contrasts the evidence-based practitioner who 'is more likely to be funded by the NHS to engage in collaborative research of direct relevance to local and national practice' with the traditional scientist-practitioner 'struggling alone and heroically to draw on and contribute to research, which occasionally results in personal guidelines to improve practice' (Milne, 1999: 5). He acknowledges that it is too early to say if the NHS research and development initiatives will adequately support EBP. The tone of the article is, however, positive about the potential benefits of EBP and encourages the profession to 'reconfigure' itself accordingly.

A letter in the same issue of *Clinical Psychology Forum* raises concerns that the government-led EBP initiative within the NHS may not be sufficiently flexible to accommodate other approaches to determining good practice. Zadik reports that he was unable to find information on EBP relevant to his clinical area (group support for carers of dementia sufferers) because the research needed to answer his questions has not been done. He lists the practical obstacles to doing research in this area and expresses the hope that representatives of the newly established National Institute for Clinical Excellence will 'accept and disseminate a broader view of what is valid evidence' (Zadik, 1999: 3). A similar objection to EBP is stated in a more recent issue of *Clinical Psychology Forum*:

> For all the disquiet it engenders, *Forum's* November 1999 themed issue on evidence-based practice is to be welcomed for giving voice to practitioners' perspectives in this important debate. It brings hopeful signs that the era of glib proclamations of professional virtue about evidence-based practice and prostletysing condescencion [*sic*] from 'ideological elites' might be replaced with more sober and truthful assessments of the nature of clinical psychology practice.... Our profession, and others too, should now recognize that just because fashionable terms like 'evidence-based practice' and 'scientist-practitioner' confer a measure of professional credibility (and sound good) they are typically not as relevant at the point of service delivery as political expediency might wish us to think. (Ørner et al., 2000: 2)

The authors go on to make a case for a 'more relevant evidence base' that looks beyond the elements of the therapeutic intervention and views outcome more holistically – considering, for example, how therapy facilitates patients' use of personal and social support (Seligman, 1995).

Niebor, Moss and Partridge argue that EBP is a discourse of 'power and restraint' as well as one of clinical rigour:

As a phrase, 'evidence-based practice' is an increasing part of the discourse of legitimacy that some of us well-armoured clinical psychologists can show to the world, and that some of us who feel more naked may fear or envy. (Niebor et al., 2000: 17)

They note that the 'evidence' that is granted legitimacy in today's NHS comes from nomothetic, meta-analytic reviews that assume comparability of research subjects. Niebor and colleagues assert that this discourse is privileged in the current political climate as a way of rationing health care while justifying it as a scientific decision, rather than a moral, economic or political one. They observe that the client may be ill-served by EBP based on data that assumes users are interchangeable units, and suggest that an *evidence-reflexive* approach should inform the determination of best practice. In this model, user and practitioner collaborate to decide what works for whom within a particular cultural and interactional context. Their advocacy of greater user involvement in decision-making is, in fact, in keeping with policy promulgated by the present government (Department of Health, 1997).

While its members have so far failed to reach consensus, the leadership of the BPS is responding to the Department of Health's clinical governance agenda by producing clinical outcome measures and protocols for risk management through its centre for Clinical Outcomes Research and Effectiveness (CORE), which was established in 1995. CORE has also collaborated with a number of other professional organisations (such as the British Association for Counselling and Psychotherapy, MIND, the Royal College of Psychiatrists and the UK Council for Psychotherapy) to produce guidelines on the acute management of schizophrenia and a document for the Department of Health entitled *Treatment Choice in Psychological Therapies and Counselling: Evidence Based Clinical Practice Guidelines* (Department of Health, 2001a). Meanwhile, the Division of Clinical Psychology (DCP) has established a committee with a remit for clinical effectiveness (QUEST). The DCP is also producing review papers (for example a review of psychological aspects of psychosis) and professional practice guidelines (for example documents on management of suspected child abuse, and management of challenging behaviour). Given the current political and economic climate, it is likely that clinical psychology, together with the other health professions, will continue down this road towards increasing proceduralisation of its work.

Hayes (1998) observes that guild forces have resisted practice guidelines in the past because they feared this would threaten their members' autonomy and status. Thus, professions have pursued credentialing of people rather than procedures. Credentialing procedures opens the process in question to scrutiny: it necessarily removes much of the indeterminacy of the knowledge that is being utilised and invites competitors from outside the profession to learn those procedures and thus acquire the credentials. This process is exemplified by the cognitive therapy training courses that have developed in Britain over the past decade and have credentialed non-psychologists/psychiatrists in a form of therapy approved by existing guidelines (for example, Department of Health, 2001a). Hayes argues:

> Psychology is in a difficult spot. It became overcommitted to psychotherapy delivery, largely giving away many hard-won prizes in that process: assessment, career counselling, child development, and so on.... Now, as the psychotherapeutic hordes move in, psychology seems to have nothing special to offer and no way to turn down the tap. (Hayes, 1998: 37)

Although Hayes is writing about the dilemmas facing clinical psychology in the United States, his observations are entirely relevant to the current situation in Britain. In fact, Hayes goes on to make the case that psychology does have something special to offer, because it is a science-based profession. Elsewhere in this paper, he expresses doubt that 'available science is...adequate to provide working answers for some questions important to the development of practice guidelines' (p. 39), but he nevertheless concludes that psychologists are best placed to develop therapy programmes linked to those guidelines, to evaluate them, to carry out training in these procedures, and to 'pick up the pieces when practice guidelines are not enough with complex cases' (p. 37). Since Hayes is a clinical psychologist himself, it is perhaps not surprising that he appears to be engaged in some special pleading for the profession.

Conclusions

Despite the success of clinical psychology's professional project, not all of its members are persuaded by the justificatory rhetoric that surrounds this enterprise. At the same time, the principles of EBP seem indisputable: '...clients should be able to assume that their treatment represents best practice, and that their therapists monitor their performance, trying to do the right things with their clients and trying to do it right' (Roth, 1999: 37). Roth, among others, has noted that the increasing emphasis on EBP has the potential to create further rifts between academic researchers and clinicians, particularly if the latter interpret EBP as politically motivated to sanction cheaper, short-term interventions without sufficient consideration of differences between clinical and research populations, or longer-term methods that have been less adequately evaluated. We will return to these issues in Chapter 7. Now we move on to examine other changes confronting the profession.

Clinical psychology in primary care

Clinical psychology posts in primary care first appeared in the mid-1970s (McAllister and Phillip, 1975), but the real growth in primary care psychology has occurred during the past decade. The model of clinical psychology in primary care is still evolving and currently operates in different locations at one of three levels. At its most traditional, primary care work means the clinical work resulting from referrals from the primary care team, usually the GP. At this level, the site where clients are seen is not considered significant and is generally a hospital outpatient clinic. The next level of primary care psychology service delivers assessment and therapy for clients in GP practices, although the psychologists who are doing this work are still very much part of a hospital-based psychology department or community team. In the third level of the primary care model, the service is offered to clients in GP practices by a combination of clinical psychologists and other providers of psychological therapies, such as counsellors, nurse therapists, counselling psychologists and health psychologists. At this level, clinical psychologists and other mental health workers are fully integrated into the primary care team. Clinical psychologists may or may not have managerial/supervisory responsibility for the other mental health workers in the teams. However, they are likely to be involved in provision of training and consultancy for other team members, and take an active part in service development. The evolution of primary care psychology can be summarised as a progression from the first to the third level described above (Day and Wren, 1994).

Within clinical psychology, the shift in emphasis from secondary to primary care has been influenced by a number of factors. Kat (1994) argues that clinical psychologists are uniquely suited to understanding 'disturbances of the normal processes of managing one's health and life' that result in individuals presenting in primary care. Growing recognition of the value of psychological therapies (Paykel and Priest, 1992) has coincided with recent health policy initiatives encouraging decentralisation of services to increase their accessibility (Department of Health, 1999a). GPs have become more influential in decisions about service provision, and became direct purchasers of services through the fundholding schemes that emerged in the early 1990s. Even though fundholding is now being wound down following the change from a Conservative to a Labour government, GPs continue to exert considerable influence on the services that are prioritised and funded within an NHS 'which will increasingly reflect the psychosocial orientation of primary care and public health, rather than the biomedical orientation of the hospital service' (McPherson and Baty, 2000). Since the majority of psychological disorders continue to be managed in primary care (Goldberg and Huxley, 1992), access to suitable mental health services is and always has been a priority for GPs.

One important consequence of clinical psychology's growth in primary care is that it represents a further stage in the profession's separation and independence from psychiatry. In some areas of the country, clinical psychology departments are now managed by Primary Care Trusts and are therefore organisationally separate from the psychiatric services, which remain in Acute Trusts. At least one clinical psychology service (a large department covering the whole of Fife) has taken a further step down this road and is now managed by a local health care co-operative (similar to the primary care groups in England). This is a very recent development but has so far proved immensely fruitful in gaining increased resources for the service.

The definition of 'suitable mental health services' is the subject of debate, even among GPs themselves. Medlik (1999) surveyed 100 GPs with direct experience of working with clinical psychologists in primary care. With a 50 per cent response rate, she found that the majority wanted clinical psychology services to be provided in their own surgeries, with the second-best option being 'sharing psychological resources with other practices at a central community primary care location' and little enthusiasm for hospital-based services. In addition to one-to-one therapy, the GPs were keen for the psychologists to offer group therapy for particular problems, consultancy on case management to members of the primary health care team (PHCT), and training for the PHCT. There were divided opinions about the value of clinical psychologists being involved in PHCT development and business meetings.

Baty, Blakey, McPherson and Peaker (2001) suggest that the sort of clinical psychology services that GPs want can best be judged by the decisions made by PHCTs while they were fund-holders in the 1990s. The authors analysed the decisions of 26 practices across three health boards in Scotland, serving both rural and urban communities and representing the full spectrum of social class. They concluded that fundholders wanted: (1) the pro-vision of psychological services, on site, by a 'named' clinician; (2) the opportunity to determine, in collaboration with the named clinical psychologist, the goals, nature and standards of the service provided for each practice; (3) to abolish traditional waiting lists in favour of early assessment, even if this meant limiting the number of referrals; (4) to utilise the named clinical psychologist for assess-ment/screening of all referred patients, with the expectation that he/she would refer relatively few individuals on to specialist clinical psychology services. The practices differed regarding the sort of cases they wished the clinical psychologists to pick up. Some pri-oritised service users with significant mental health problems that would benefit from a relatively short intervention (less than eight sessions), while others prioritised patients with severe and endur-ing problems who were making considerable demands on the rest of the PHCT. In terms of the clinical psychologist's contributions to the PHCT, Baty and colleagues concluded that these fundhold-ers did not consider training, consultancy and service development work to be as important as assessment and treatment of patients. They also noted that these GPs did not opt for the cheapest service, given that some had the choice of less expensive nurse-led mental health services.

Papworth (2000) describes delivery of primary care psychology, in conjunction with counselling services, in north-east England over a three-year period. He reports high referrer and client satisfaction with the service and consistently short delays before initial assess-ment (an average wait of one month). Papworth describes the ben-efits of shifting the administration of the service to the primary care setting: it simplifies procedures and 'exerts a degree of homeostatic control' over referrals as GPs have open access to waiting lists and regulate referrals accordingly. Finally, Papworth reports the success of joint projects with other members of the PHCT (for example, a tranquilliser withdrawal programme) and primary prevention work undertaken with a health visitor addressing the needs of mothers with specified problems.

Commenting on the development of clinical psychology in pri-mary care within a devolved Scotland, McPherson and Baty (2000) observe that the Scottish Office White Paper *Designed to Care* (1997) encouraged the development of extended primary care teams (as in level 3 of the primary care model described earlier: see p. 89) and of clinical specialities within primary care. They note that development of such specialities would provide an intermediate level of service between the generalist skills of the primary care clinician and the input provided by hospital-based services. These primary care specialities may be defined by problem area (such as eating disorders), or by client group.

Boyle, Lindsay and McPherson (1997) provide an example of the latter, describing a primary care development initiative that supplied funding for a one-year programme to evaluate a primary-care-based clinical child psychology service. The service was established in two GP practices in rural Scotland and was designed as an alternative to existing secondary services that were perceived by GPs as expensive and insufficiently accessible or responsive to the needs of their patients and PHCTs. In consultation with the practices, four objectives were identified for the service: (1) provision of liaison and consultancy work involving members of the PHCT, as well as other health and education staff; (2) health education and promotion; (3) staff education and training; and (4) direct clinical work. The authors conclude that the new service addressed a hitherto unmet need (referrals totalled 79 during the year, compared with eight the previous year, and the increase was made up of individuals with significant difficulties); had a lower non-attendance rate than traditional secondary-care-based services; fostered better interdisciplinary and inter-agency work, and was preferred by both patients and PHCT members.

One of the most challenging aspects of the developments in primary care work is the growing emphasis on *skill mix*. Ten years ago, Miller (1994) observed that increasing numbers of counsellors were being employed in primary care, in parallel with a growing trend for departments of clinical psychology to employ therapists of varying backgrounds, such as nurse therapists trained in behaviour therapy or cognitive therapy, counselling psychologists and health psychologists. Miller argued that these developments had taken place for three reasons: there were insufficient numbers of qualified clinical psychologists to meet the demand for psychological therapy within the NHS; in some situations, purchasers perceived these other therapists as less expensive than clinical psychologists; and the increasing professionalisation of counselling had raised its profile and enhanced its credibility with purchasers. Given these changes, Miller expressed support for the practice of employing non-clinical psychologists within clinical psychology departments and cautioned the profession against mimicking the very behaviour it has sometimes attributed to psychiatry: attempts to block the development of other professions in order to retain dominance in the field. He concluded that closer working relationships between clinical psychologists and other providers of psychological therapy would produce a more comprehensive and cohesive service for users and purchasers, and ensure proper supervision and accountability of staff.

Since that paper was written, the skill-mix model has become increasingly prevalent (see for example: Green, 1994; Collins and Murray, 1995; Hall, 1997; Heller, 1997; Miller, 1997; Shillitoe and Hall, 1997; Kemp and Thwaites, 1998). An independent opinion on the organisation of psychological services (MAS, 1996) recommended that they should be provided by pluralistic departments employing different disciplines that were centrally managed, and advised that they should be delivered in a range of locations. Furthermore, Paxton (2000) notes that the current ethos in the NHS makes multidisciplinary and multi-agency working almost essential if NHS research and development funding is being sought. Some clinical psychology departments are employing therapists of different backgrounds purely to share the primary care work, while in other departments the skill mix has a broader remit. For example, one department in the north-east of England has been reorganised to 'have lead responsibility within the Trust for psychological therapies and research' and includes clinical psychologists, counsellors, nurse therapists and art therapists (Paxton, 2000). This sort of reorganisation places additional demands on staff with managerial responsibilities, and a recent review of staff roles and training in the mental health sector concluded that clinical psychologists should receive additional training in management, consultancy, staff facilitation and communication skills (Sainsbury Centre for Mental Health, 1997).

Community psychology

In the previous section we quoted the observation by McPherson and Baty (2000) that the NHS is increasingly adopting the 'psychosocial orientation of primary care and public health, rather than the biomedical orientation of the hospital service'. Some clinical psychologists are committed to a position that places still greater emphasis on social factors as contributors to individual distress. Community psychology emerged in the mid-1960s, born out of the social justice movement in the United States. Its advocates approach individual distress from a social and environmental perspective and promote an alternative to the traditional intrapsychic emphasis of psychological therapies offered in healthcare settings. Community psychologists are explicit about the need for social change and expect to play an active part in the process. Their contributions to change will vary: community psychologists include clinical, educational and academic psychologists.

While community psychology has existed as a division of the American Psychological Association since 1967, it has not yet achieved this status in Britain and there is no recognised career path for its practitioners in this country. However, there is a growing network of community psychologists (including clinicians) who continue to promote this approach, and the *Journal of Community and Applied Social Psychology* was founded in 1991 to facilitate interdisciplinary discussion of sociopsychological theory and practice. The mission statement of the journal was clear in the editorial of the first issue, which contained the assertion that 'psychological ideas and practices should help remove exploitation and oppression from people's lives' (Mansell et al., 1991).

Orford (1998) acknowledges that there is not yet a unified community psychology theory for clinical psychologists to embrace or reject, but suggests that the following principles capture the aims of its proponents in Britain:

The task of community psychology is then to help people:

1. Understand the connection between the social and economic reality of their lives and their states of health and well-being.
2. Join with others with similar realities to give voice to this understanding.
3. Engage in collective action to change these realities. (Orford, 1998: 10)

This brief reflects both ideological and pragmatic concerns. Community psychologists believe that the scale of mental health problems confronting us as a result of the 'psychologically toxic social environments' we inhabit makes intervention at the individual level impractical. A comparison between community psychology and traditional psychological services therefore yields discrepancies in a number of dimensions, including aetiological assumptions about the genesis of individual distress, and attitudes towards service planning, delivery and evaluation (see Table 5.1).

The nature of the relationship between community psychology and clinical psychology is subject to debate. Fryer (1998) contends that community psychology is located outside 'orthodox experimental and clinical psychology', which he refers to as 'institutional psychology':

Table 5.1 *Comparison of community psychology and traditional psychological approaches*

	Community psychology approach	Traditional psychological services
Aetiological assumptions	Environmental/ecological explanations of psychological distress	Intrapsychic explanations of psychological distress
Planning & development	Co-ordinated, proactive, linked with unmet needs and populations at risk	Individual services reactive to NHS professionals
Location of intervention	Communities	Institutional, mental health settings
Level of intervention	Socially or geographically defined communities and groups	Individual clients
Strategies of interventions	Preventive, brief, collaborative interventions which may be aimed at large numbers of people	Reactive, formal, specialised psychotherapy
Service delivery	Indirect contact via education and consultation	Direct services to clients
Staffing	Mental health professionals, other professional and lay people	Mental health professionals
Research/evaluation	Community led, action orientated	Professionally led, often for academic purposes

Source: From Bostock, 1998, with reference to Rappaport, 1977

The absence of community psychology from most UK psychology syllabuses can be explained in part because many institutional psychologists and their protectionist organisations misrepresent community psychology as operating beyond the legitimate realm of the discipline in the quasi-scientific or non-scientific territory of sociologists and politicians, mired in subjectivity and ideological bias, offering a messy compromise of naively idealistic Utopianism and political activism as academic social science. (Fryer, 1998: 46)

Certainly, there is little emphasis on community psychology in most of the existing clinical psychology training programmes, with the exception of the University of Exeter course, which has promoted this approach for many years.

Despite the absence of support from training institutions, Spence (1998) argues that community psychology is potentially 'the centre of mainstream' clinical psychology because it 'is a distillation of ideas and theories' that underpin current practice in the profession. Spence notes that clinical psychologists are increasingly aware of the importance of *context* – of understanding how the individual's environment influences his/her behaviour. The growth of systemic theories and therapies is one indication of this development. Social constructionism and the rise of pluralism have produced another paradigm shift, encouraging clinicians to be sceptical of an objective reality and become more receptive to their clients' interpretations of reality. Spence also identifies factors from the wider political context that are assisting community psychology to become mainstream: (1) there is an increasing acceptance that demand will always exceed supply of mental health services; (2) the present government has demonstrated its interest in early interventions and an approach to health that takes social factors into account; (3) conventional treatments are undergoing unprecedented scrutiny and are required to show efficacy, which opens the door for new approaches to be evaluated; (4) there is an increasing commitment to user involvement in policy-making; (5) there is growing commitment to equity of both service provision and access to services; and (6) there is increasing commitment to interagency working and partnership between agencies and the public.

Frankish (1999) concurs with Spence's view that clinical psychology is likely to become increasingly community and systems orientated. Indeed, she goes further and argues that this shift is necessary if the profession is to survive and flourish. Frankish, a senior member of the profession with experience as an officer of the DCP and a clinical director for mental health in the NHS, contends that clinical psychologists are generally not providing 'the leadership and direction in services that their comprehensive training and salary would predict'. She observes that the profession lacks influence because its members are spending most of their time doing one-to-one therapy, and accuses the profession of isolationist tendencies that are not compatible with the growing emphasis on multi-skilled, multi-disciplinary and multi-agency working within the NHS. While Frankish acknowledges the importance of individual therapy, she urges psychologists to begin using the other skills they acquire during training to lead, co-ordinate and train other workers; to shape services (health, education and social); and to become more involved in developing innovative care packages for people with chronic difficulties.

It is our view that the tenets of community psychology *will* become more influential in shaping the direction of the profession. One of the forces that will drive this development is the current political commitment to social inclusion, stated unequivocally in the *National Service Framework for Mental Health*:

Health and Social Services should promote mental health for all, work with individuals and communities, combat discrimination against groups with mental health problems and promote their social inclusion. (Standard One of the NSF; Department of Health, 1999a)

Commitment to social inclusion and increasing user involvement in clinical psychology service provision assumes a collaborative journey for clinicians and service users, with each group respected for the expertise it can contribute. However, while this ethos appears to be gaining credibility, some psychologists fear that the proposed reforms to the Mental Health Act of 1983 will lead the profession in a contrary direction, as its members assume greater responsibility for social control. In the following section we will consider the implications of these proposals.

Reform of the Mental Health Acts

Reforms to mental health legislation are currently under consideration in Scotland, England and Wales[1]. In December 2000, the government issued a joint Department of Health and Home Office White Paper suggesting a series of reforms to the 1983 Mental Health Act.[2] The White Paper is in two parts: the first part deals with compulsory treatment for individuals with a 'mental disorder', while the second part is largely concerned with individuals who are deemed to pose a risk to others. The proposals in the White Paper sparked a number of concerns among clinical psychologists, and other professional and non-statutory bodies. If the proposals become law, they will apply to children, adults with learning disabilities, and older adults, as well as adults of working age (for a more detailed discussion of these issues, see Cooke, Harper and Kinderman, 2001, 2002; Cooke, Kinderman and Harper, 2002; Kinderman, 2002).

Individuals covered by Part 1 of the White Paper must have a 'mental disorder', and be either at risk of serious harm that could be addressed through a compulsory care plan, or such a care plan must be in their 'best interests'. While many psychologists welcome the move away from the narrow definitions of diagnostic categories, there are concerns about the lack of functional criteria to clarify the term 'mental disorder' and the difficulty of establishing what is in someone's 'best interests'. A recent survey of clinical psychologists reported that the majority (87 per cent from a sample of 681; Cooke, Kinderman and Harper, 2002) hold the view that 'superseding all other considerations, a Mental Health Act should only apply to people who are unable ... to give or withhold valid consent'. This view is shared by the Royal College of Psychiatrists, the House of Commons Select Committee on Health, MIND, and members of the Mental Health Alliance, among others (Kinderman, 2002).

Part 2 of the White Paper allows for the detention of people who are assessed as 'dangerous and having a severe personality disorder' (DSPD). Again, the majority (84–99 per cent in a series of related questions) of clinical psychologists surveyed believed that access to psychological treatment for people who have exhibited violent behaviour should not depend on their being assessed as personality disordered; that mental health legislation is not an appropriate vehicle for imposing control on people who are capable of making valid decisions for themselves; and that risk assessment is both unreliable and likely to lead to significant numbers of individuals being detained unnecessarily (Cooke, Kinderman & Harper, 2002).

Clinical psychologists have not only been concerned about the scope of the new Act, but they have also been debating anticipated changes to their role. Two specific proposals would allow for the involvement of clinical psychologists in the detention/compulsory treatment process. First, approved social workers will be replaced by 'approved' or 'suitably trained' mental health professionals (including psychologists) as co-ordinators of the preliminary examination of patients to determine suitability for compulsory treatment/ detention. Second, it is proposed that the current Responsible Medical Officer (RMO) role should be replaced with that of 'Clinical Supervisor'. Clinical supervisors will be responsible for overseeing the compulsory care plans that will replace the present system of compulsory detention under a 'section' of the Mental Health Act. The White Paper explicitly states that a clinical supervisor could be a consultant psychologist or a psychiatrist. In the survey of DCP members, one-third of respondents thought that the profession should resist this proposed extension of the clinical psychologist's role, although half of the sample said they would be willing to act as a clinical supervisor if given appropriate training (Cooke, Kinderman & Harper, 2002). Thus, the profession remains split over this issue at the present time. In the following section we will summarise some of the views on both sides.

Some clinical psychologists have viewed these proposals as a positive development. Levenson (2001) argues that the development of new roles such as Clinical Supervisor would not necessarily 'detract' from therapeutic relationships and, indeed, could increase psychology's contribution to the assessment and treatment of these individuals. Levenson also suggests that the new role 'could enhance the status of the profession'. Black (2001) identifies another benefit of psychologists assuming the Clinical Supervisor role: it would prevent RMOs from making decisions on behalf of other professions. He gives the example of RMOs detaining individuals so they can receive psychological treatment that psychologists might deem inappropriate. Conversely, individuals have been refused admission by RMOs when a psychologist would have assessed them as treatable. Black also cites the example of people being discharged or transferred to another treatment facility without consultation with the psychologists involved when they are in the middle of a treatment programme. Finally, he predicts that clinical supervisors will be even more accountable than RMOs: under the new Act, mental health review tribunals will be able to review not only the grounds for continued compulsory treatment, but also the original grounds for the treatment order.

Levenson's assertion that clinical psychologists could act as clinical supervisors without jeopardising their role as therapist and advocate for clients has been challenged by several respondents in the profession's trade journal, *Clinical Psychology* (Cattrall et al., 2001; Diamond, 2001; Markman, 2002; Holmes, 2002)[3]. Diamond responds to Levenson's remarks thus:

> Unlike Levenson ... it is my view that such roles would turn clinical psychologists into moral arbiters with law enforcing functions. Once this happens, we become decision makers of what is and what is not considered to be socially acceptable behaviour. More importantly, in my view, we stop being clinical psychologists. (Diamond, 2001: 9)

He goes on to question whether any increase in status that members of the profession might experience as a result of assuming the Clinical Supervisor role would be 'either desirable or appropriate'. Diamond argues that clinical psychology already 'mimics psychiatry too closely' and he urges the profession instead to work more closely with service users to develop 'more meaningful and appropriate services'. Mental health services and clinical psychology are, he suggests, at a crossroad: we can choose the path towards social inclusion or head towards a punitive and coercive role in pursuit of social control. This view is echoed by Cattrall and colleagues, who argue that compulsory treatment is unethical and ineffective. They voice the concern that if the profession, as a whole, accepts the Clinical Supervisor role, it may become increasingly difficult for individual clinical psychologists to decline it – given the national shortage of psychiatrists. In conclusion, they remind readers that clinical psychology exists to help service users and yet no user groups have, they claim, expressed support for the proposed reforms (Cattrall et al., 2001).

Holmes (2002), writing from the perspective of a clinical psychologist who has worked in a regional secure unit and a community mental health team with people who have been sectioned under the 1983 Act, raises some additional concerns about the proposed reforms. Like others, he questions the effectiveness of compulsory treatment, but he goes on to question whether compulsion reduces risk of self-harm or harm to others, citing evidence that prediction of risk is not reliable (Crawford, 2000). Holmes also challenges the argument by supporters of the proposals that psychologists would employ the Act 'more humanely' than other professionals. He observes that social psychologists such as Milgram have shown that the behaviour of individuals is highly susceptible to change under the influence of a new role: assuming a coercive role can generate coercive and even abusive behaviour. Finally, he cautions that the proposed reforms could split the profession, with one group accepting or even welcoming the 'expert, paternalistic' role of Clinical Supervisor, and the rest of the profession refusing to do Mental Health Act work on ethical grounds.

In light of the recent survey of DCP members (Cooke, Kinderman and Harper, 2002) it seems as though Holmes has legitimate cause for concern in anticipating that the proposed reforms to the Mental Health Act could split the profession if they become a reality. Assumption of these formal powers under the Act is likely to align clinical psychologists (at least those acting as clinical supervisors) more closely with the social control functions of the psy complex, while developments in primary care and community psychology are simultaneously weakening links of other members of the profession with the traditional power bases of the health professions.

Despite the implications of these developments for further segmentation in the profession, it is our view that the likely extension of our role under the new Mental Health Act would be legitimate. If psychiatrists already have dirty hands from doing the dirty work of detaining people under the old Mental Health Act, psychologists have so far been the beneficiaries of being sidelined in past legislation. This is arguably why many psychologists are now offended by the incipient Clinical Supervisor role: the indignation reflects our lack of legal responsibility to date. We inherit a moral high ground of benign voluntarism, which we are reluctant to leave. But is this position of refusing legal responsibility self-evidently politically defensible? If we live in a society with mental health law that can offend civil liberties and damage people, are we not *already* party to this problem? The mental health system is governed by rules of coercion and weak advocacy. If we work in the NHS, the state pays us for being part of that system, whatever role is given to us within its division of labour. Why should psychologists claim the luxury of eschewing this dirty work? Somebody has to do it. Why not us?

Mental Health (Scotland) Bill

In Scotland, the situation regarding proposed mental health legislation is very different. Here, the process of reform has generated the Mental Health (Scotland) Bill and this is currently being considered by the Health and Community Care Committee of the Scottish Parliament. The Division of Clinical Psychology–Scottish Branch (DCP–SB) has reacted favourably to some of the proposals in the legislation: for example, the possibility of compulsory treatment in the community, the introduction of a new independent tribunal system to deal with treatment orders, and an increased emphasis on involving patients and their families in the decision-making. However, DCP–SB has also expressed some reservations about the draft legislation and has signed up to the 'Let's Get It Right' campaign with a number of mental health charities and action groups to lobby for amendments. As in England and Wales, there are concerns about the inadequate definition of 'personality disorder' in the Bill. However, while clinical psychologists south of the border are debating the merits of an enhanced role for clinical psychologists under their new mental health Act, psychologists in Scotland are concerned at being sidelined by the Mental Health (Scotland) Bill.

Significantly, the Bill identifies different forms of medical treatment for mental disorder but does not mention psychological treatment; and does not identify a role for clinical psychologists in a range of related activities, such as assessment of psychological needs, provision/supervision of psychological treatments, risk assessment and assessment of capacity for informed consent. There are no proposals in this legislation for the role of Responsible Medical Officer to be replaced by that of Clinical Supervisor, so clinical psychologists will not assume the powers of detention north of the border. While the DCP–SB does not seek statutory powers for its members, it is lobbying for amendments to the draft that will direct RMOs and mental health officers involved in compulsory treatment orders to seek a report from a clinical psychologist when issues requiring psychological expertise arise.

Conclusions

In this chapter we have considered some of the ways in which the work of clinical psychologists in Britain is likely to change in the near future. In Chapter 6 we will return to our discussion of Larson's professional project and consider how clinical psychology has sustained, and arguably enhanced, its marketability through promotion of its expertise. Our final chapter will then examine both the internal and external relationships that define our profession in Britain and will conclude by summarising some of the theoretical debates that continue to stimulate and at times divide us.

Notes

1 Northern Ireland is also reviewing its legislation but the scope of our book is limited to Great Britain.

2 The proposals in the White Paper apply only to England and Wales. In Scotland the process of reform has generated the Mental Health (Scotland) Bill to supersede the Mental Health (Scotland) Act 1984. The Bill is currently being considered in committee by the Scottish Parliament.

3 *Clinical Psychology Forum* prior to May 2001.

6
EXPERTS AND EXPERTISE

Modern professions can be understood and depicted in a variety of ways. In the first two chapters we explored two of these by addressing the history of clinical psychology and its knowledge base. This chapter pursues a third method of understanding, focusing on professions as interest groups operating in a social system, which claim a unique mandate based upon specialist knowledge or expertise. This broad approach begins with a discussion of the sociology of the professions and, specifically for our purposes here, studies of health care systems and the role of clinical professions within them. After this we move into an examination of expertise from the perspectives of cognitive psychology and studies of organisational behaviour.

Clinical psychology and expertise

The contributions of the sociology of professions help us, to some degree, in understanding clinical psychology. However, the advice is broad, varied and at times contradictory. Clinical psychology (like other professions) is constituted by a set of practices and knowledge claims which are rich and complex and so open to a variety of interpretations and analyses. Thus, each approach from the sociology of the professions can find some empirical basis for its preferred form of understanding. For example, clinical psychologists sometimes *do* act in a way which suggests that they are interested in excluding competitors, confirming the neo-Weberian perspective. The Marxian model (alluding to contradictions in the new middle class) also fits to some extent: the profession does serve the interests of social stability (and is thus, in a broad sense, an agent of social regulation for the employing capitalist state). At the same time, the profession is a workforce and so its individual members, by and large, are wage slaves. Equally, clinical psychology is gendered and so a feminist analysis tells us something about the interests of the profession. Similarly, the poststructuralist accounts are persuasive in other respects – the profession does seem to be part of a 'psy complex', in which overlapping forms of practice are shared with others in the mental health industry.

Even the trait and functionalist positions, within the sociology of the professions, provide useful material for critical debate. Because the positions celebrate and promote the self-serving accounts of professional leaders, critical onlookers have access to elaborate examples of professional rhetoric (Simons, 1984).

The partial fit of each approach is reminiscent of the blind men and the elephant. Each, in his own way, touches and truly describes an aspect of the animal but none of them can capture the whole picture. It may be possible to provide a more coherent view of the profession as an interest group in society if we start with another concept: expertise. The advantage of this concept is that it allows us to include the insights of the competing models from the sociology of the professions (such as those noted above), while at the same time staying close to the particular details of clinical psychology. The latter is important because the subdivision of middle-class labour in modern societies means that we are all now surrounded by a vast *range* of experts, each with particular claims and peculiar norms of practice.

The sociological approaches noted above seem to have conceived of experts as forming very broad categories (the 'new middle class', 'mature professions', 'semi-professions', etc.). When we delve into the detail of specific groups of experts in these categories, unique features emerge within broader trends that connect them with other groups. Studying professions is like scanning a broad area with a telescope. Studying expertise takes a bit of the view and gets closer to its empirical character.

What then is the *particular expertise* being claimed by the profession of clinical psychology? This can be summarised in two ways. First we can list the traditional functional activities which clinical psychologists have claimed for themselves as unique: providing psychological formulations of individuals or groups; carrying out psychological interventions ('therapies'); training others in psychological technologies of assessment or intervention; and research. However, as noted earlier, this list overlaps with the expertise of others in the psy complex. For example, medical psychotherapists and nurse therapists are all involved in the first three activities on the list. As for research, this is carried out by most of the professions defined at a graduate level in the health service.

Nonetheless, when the Division of Clinical Psychology came to define the profession in 2001 in a short document, *The Core Purpose and Philosophy of the Profession* (DCP, 2001b), it held firm to this traditional list of functions (assessment, formulation, intervention, evaluation, and research). Moreover, it did so within an ethos of 'scientific humanism'. This term was used by Richards (1983), when he studied the values and interests emerging in British clinical psychology after the Second World War and connotes the idea that practitioners aspire to use science in the service of human improvement. Thus, the profession's philosophy is, for now, as follows:

The work of clinical psychologists is based on the fundamental acknowledgment that all people have the same human value and the right to be treated as unique individuals. Clinical psychologists will treat all people – both clients and colleagues – with dignity and respect and will work with them collaboratively as equal partners towards the achievement of mutually agreed goals. In doing this, clinical psychologists will adhere to and be guided by explicit and public statements of the ethical principles that underpin their work. (DCP, 2001b: 2)

The document goes on to announce the profession's purpose:

Clinical psychology aims to reduce psychological distress and to enhance and promote psychological well-being by the systematic application of knowledge derived from psychological theory and data. (DCP, 2001b: 2)

A second way of defining expertise in the profession, implied in this statement, is to identify a feature of the profession which is *not* shared by others. This method of defining expertise can be found most readily in the MPAG review in 1988 when Derek Mowbray produced his hierarchy of psychological knowledge, with clinical psychologists alone offering level 3 skills (see Chapter 1). What is interesting about this is that Mowbray produced a credible rationale for *psychologists* in this regard. In doing so he did not seal off clinical from other branches of the discipline. For our purposes, for example, we could look at the role of counselling psychologists or (non-clinical) forensic psychologists. They too might now claim to offer Mowbray's level 3 skills. Similarly, it could be argued that the DCP's statement on the purpose of the profession identifies the claimed expertise of psychologists, but not necessarily that of clinical psychologists alone.

The DCP document cited above deals with the threat posed by other psychologists in a tangential way. It does not explicitly concede that forensic, health and counselling psychologists are in direct competition with clinical psychology. Instead it argues that the latter should be the key adviser to employers (in Britain, still primarily the NHS) regarding the recruitment and deployment of other groups:

Currently clinical psychologists are probably in the best position to advise on the psychological needs of the communities they serve and on how such needs might be fulfilled. Because of their historic position in the NHS and their numbers (they are currently the largest single group of applied psychologists) they can advise on what sorts of psychologists are required to fulfil which psychological needs. This will include ensuring that different types of applied psychological skill are properly represented in the portfolio of services offered. (DCP, 2001b: 7)

This statement is a coded way of persuading employers that clinical psychologists should mediate, or regulate, any local developments in the growth and role of counselling and other non-clinical psychologists. However, the disciplinary proximity of counselling psychology to clinical psychology, in terms of its academic background, routine functions and work settings (counselling psychologists also mainly practise in the NHS) poses a peculiar challenge to the boundaries and expertise of clinical psychologists. A formal position statement was issued, in July 2001, by the Division of Counselling Psychology. The statement quoted above from the Division of Clinical Psychology emerged in January 2001. This might prompt us to speculate if one provoked the other.

Given the relatively new status of the Division of Counselling Psychology (it has existed only since 1995), its statement did not claim to be 'comprehensive or definitive' (Division of Counselling Psychology, 2001: 1). Despite this tentative stance, the document included guidance to employers which is remarkably reminiscent of that offered by clinical psychologists. For example, we are told that qualification in counselling psychology entails undergraduate work in psychology followed by a three-year postgraduate training. The list of specific competencies enumerated in the Division of Counselling Psychology's statement also includes assessment, formulation, therapy, supervision of others and research and development, while the list of settings in which the two applied branches of psychology operate is virtually the same. Finally, we are told that counselling psychologists are 'competent deliverers of evidence-based psychological therapy'. Indeed, an outsider fresh to the documents would be hard pressed to differentiate the self-descriptions issued by these two divisions of the British Psychological Society.

This process of pushing more and more for defining features of expertise reminds us that the devil is in the detail of professional life, and clear generalisations from models offered by the differing schools within the sociology of the professions are not easy to make. Not only do clinical psychologists share some activities with non-psychologists, they also share them with non-clinical psychologists. Despite the claims of Mowbray and the Division of Clinical Psychology, there is no fail-safe way of permanently marking off the expertise of the profession from the work of other occupational groups. This seems to give support to the poststructuralist notion of a psy complex, with substantial functional overlap existing between mental health workers emerging from a variety of training routes.

Moving on from the ways in which a close scrutiny of the profession provides us with rich food for thought about the problem of *defining* clinical psychology, such an intimate examination also reveals other peculiar contradictions. As discussed in Chapter 2, the knowledge base of the profession is highly contested. Thus, for every example of a defining point of consensus for the profession (for instance, level 3 skills), a sceptic can find a subject on which clinical psychologists profoundly disagree. It is well known in the folklore of the profession that the collective noun for the profession is 'a disagreement'. If a clinical psychologist with a psychodynamic orientation were asked to formulate a complex case, his/her view would be at odds with a cognitive-behavioural formulation of the same case, and one clinician's persuasive eclecticism is another's hopeless confusion. For these reasons, some clinical psychologists openly concede that their primary identity might be as a particular type of *therapist* rather than having much sense of connection with others in their profession (Mollon, 1989).

A related, contradictory feature of the profession is that its knowledge base has a contested core orthodoxy of scientific rationality (hence the attempt to define the profession by the role of the 'scientist-practitioner'). However, the circles of dissent, which swirl around and challenge this core identity, are now well documented. There are recurring protests within the profession that the current cognitive-behavioural orthodoxy does not respect the psychodynamic tradition in its midst or, indeed, any of the other competing perspectives. In the 1950s, when behaviour therapy emerged as the dominant theoretical and therapeutic approach (foreshadowing CBT), champions of personal construct theory (PCT) reacted publicly against behaviourist hegemony, although PCT has never been widely practised in the UK (Bannister and Fransella, 1970). Divisions in the clinic reflect deeper unresolved tensions in the academy between objectivism and subjectivism in the discipline of psychology.

The knowledge base of clinical psychology is not only contested, but it has also been accused of being overly masculine by feminists in its midst. This can be traced back to the differentiation of psychology from philosophy in the academy, with a shift from inner reflection to empirical observation. However, this empiricist emphasis in the profession has been a precarious orthodoxy, with recurring doubts being expressed by critics about therapeutic models (for example psychodynamic and humanistic critiques of behaviourism) and methodology (the advocacy of qualitative methods as a replacement for or adjunct to quantitative methods). These criticisms are not exclusive to feminist commentators, but they can certainly be found in the writing of feminist clinical psychologists (see, for example, Ussher, 1991). Feminism, like other recent social movements, has placed experience and biographical context in a central position. By contrast, the masculine orthodoxy of psychology (traditionally reflected in clinical work) has favoured scientific expertise derived from aggregate data, the application of evidence-based techniques to *a priori* categories (like 'panic disorder') and has distrusted biographical forms of psychology and qualitative methods.

Feminists have been more generally sceptical of expertise in the health professions, which they accuse of being patriarchal in their epistemological assumptions and of being preoccupied with pathologising ordinary female experience and action. In particular, feminists argue that patriarchal knowledge (which the objectivist orthodoxy of much academic psychology exemplifies) creates a double barrier to women. First, it creates the conditions under which women adopt masculine knowledge as a condition of entrance and advancement in the mental health professions. Second, that form of knowledge frames female experience in a hard and overly rational way in terms of the clients served or targeted by the profession. For example, one feminist analyst argues that 'questions about knowledge are implicated in all aspects of women's oppression' (Code, 1991: 176).

More recent feminist analyses of psychological expertise have, because of their focus on knowledge, incorporated a Foucauldian view of power. Rather than seeing this as a knowing conspiracy of male experts against their female clients, they now concede that power is dispersed and dominant discourses privilege some accounts of reality and silence others. In relation to clinical psychology, women predominate numerically but they may provide little resistance to forms of knowledge, which have patriarchal roots in Victorian laboratory life (Ussher, 1991). The view held by followers of Foucault is the mirror image of those who generate professional rhetoric (for example Parry, 1989; Marzillier and Hall, 1999) to advance the interests of the profession. If it is the job of the latter to *construct* a case for the peculiar expertise of clinical psychologists, it is the job of postmodern critics to *deconstruct* such professional knowledge and action (Parker, 1999). The work of the latter has sought to explore how 'psychological technologies' or 'technologies of the self' emerged during modernity to lock social problems inside individuals (Rose, 1985).

According to postmodernist critics, this occurred via the confluence of disciplinary expertise (promoted by professionals and accepted by their clients) and personal conversations eclipsing the religious confessional in an increasingly secularised age. This is explained by Foucault:

> The confession has spread its effects far and wide. It plays a part in justice, medicine, education, family relations, in the most ordinary affairs of everyday life and in the most solemn rites: one confesses one's crimes, one's sins, one's thoughts and desires, one's illnesses and troubles; one goes about telling with the greatest precision whatever is the most difficult to tell. (Foucault, 1991: 59)

For Foucault, disciplinary expertise was increasingly defined by rationality (its own internal rationality and that negotiated in its clientele). Those on the outside of the discipline learned to accept and respect disciplinary knowledge. For the Foucauldians, this pact between the expert and their client offered to liberate the latter and increase their autonomy but was selling a false promise. Instead, they argue, disciplinary knowledge creates a form of restricted experience. This oppression is not imposed coercively (as it was for certified lunatics in the asylum system) but is negotiated voluntarily when talking treatments are offered to, and gratefully received by, individuals. This position creates a tension in postmodern analyses of mental health work. On the one hand, postmodernism provides a framework for *doing* therapy, albeit in a new liberal client-centred way that is, ironically, another form of expertise. On the other hand, it seems to provide the justification for clients and potential clients to *refuse* to engage with or accept this expertise, which threatens to inscribe a pre-formed reality restrictively on to individual clients. This ambivalence is explored by a variety of authors in Parker (1999).

Within this postmodern frame of understanding about psychological expertise, clinical psychology emerged along with other occupational groups in the psy complex. The great bulk of its activity operates within a voluntary context. For this reason, the profession quite understandably argues that its aim is 'collaborative' (see the DCP statement of its philosophy cited on p. 104), although a minority of its members work in secure environments and some of its work deals with the assessment and management of risky behaviour.

While the account of expertise given from a poststructuralist perspective has much to commend it, it has its own weaknesses (Pilgrim, 2000). For example, its emphasis on discourses or discursive practices rejects plausible insights from other approaches, such as the neo-Weberian emphasis on professional dominance and social closure. Furthermore, it argues that expertise *produces* mental health problems and that the latter are a by-product of professional activity. In fact, there is ample evidence that sadness, fear and madness existed prior to the emergence of the psy complex. Also, as we note above, it is not clear whether postmodern accounts are being offered as a basis for rejecting or renewing psychological expertise.

Finally, poststructuralist accounts are idealist (in the philosophical sense). Consequently the preoccupation with ideas-in-actions (discursive practices) and representations of, or silences about, reality (discourses) leave the approach vulnerable to accusations of anti-realism and nihilism. Is there no materiality to psychological distress and dysfunction? If we can tell any story about such a reality, will any story do? Despite these caveats, the critical emphasis of deconstruction gives us a useful framework to address mental health work sceptically.

Reflexive lessons from cognitive psychology

Given that expertise entails, or is constituted by, the thought and actions of experts, it is little surprise that cognitive psychology has offered its own perspective on the topic. This provides us with a particular opportunity for disciplinary reflexivity: maybe psychology can account for its own forms of expert application, such as clinical psychology. Hoffman (1998), summarising the contribution of cognitive psychology to an understanding of expertise, suggests three defining cognitive features to consider.

First, expertise entails a *developmental process*. The shift occurs from ignorance or superficial and literal understandings to complex, confident and reflexive ones. The speed and capacity of people to move along this dimension of knowledge acquisition varies from person to person. Indeed, the fact that professions select or screen candidates for entry to their ranks suggests that early probabilistic judgements are made about the aptitude of neophytes to make such a developmental shift, within the socialisation period offered by training. When psychology graduates apply for, but are rejected by, training courses, in part this reflects judgements by qualified senior colleagues about their lack of aptitude to develop. Hoffman makes the point that time *per se* may not bring about developmental changes in expertise. Some individuals develop quickly, others slowly or they may never progress in their expertise.

Of course, expertise is not an all-or-nothing phenomenon. Rounsaville et al. (1988) illustrate this point with their findings regarding therapist training for the large, multi-centre National

Institute for Mental Health Collaborative Depression study in the USA. Eleven carefully selected, experienced therapists were offered intensive training in interpersonal therapy (IPT) for the purposes of the trial. However, despite apparently high levels of motivation, two of the 11 trainees failed to achieve competency as IPT therapists. This finding will not surprise therapists who have studied or trained in several therapeutic approaches and have discovered that some are more accessible to them than others, reflecting a variety of factors including personality and worldview (Vasco et al., 1993).

Second, expertise reflects an extensive and flexible *knowledge structure*. Novices tend to think more concretely about analytical and performative tasks within professions. Experts think in more general abstract terms and will use flexible discretion about how they perform their professional duties. With regard to clinical psychology, this reflects the level 3 skills claimed on its behalf by reviewers and professional leaders. However, studies of therapeutic outcomes do not clearly signal that these improve with the seniority of the practitioner. Instead, the picture that emerges is one of complex interactions between a number of therapist variables (including level of training, amount of experience, therapeutic orientation) and an equally diverse array of client variables that together mediate therapeutic outcome (see, for example, Bergin and Garfield, 1994).

We need to be careful about assuming that socially agreed expertise (often assumed from a practitioner's evident seniority) and effectiveness are neatly correlated. The above generalisation about knowledge structure may be more reliable when the object or target of expertise is inanimate (for example the work of meteorologists, engineers or physicists). When expertise entails a human clientele who have problems in living, then the *relational and affective* aspects of professional practice are as important as the cognitive resources of practitioners. In the clinical literature, a great deal of attention has been paid to these relational factors in analyses of the contribution of the *therapeutic relationship* to the outcome of therapy. Carl Rogers's (1957) conceptualisation of the 'necessary and sufficient' conditions for effective psychotherapy as the therapist's unconditional positive regard, genuineness and empathy provided the starting point for extensive research on the qualities of productive alliances between therapists and their clients. Numerous investigations into the effects of relationship variables in therapy have consistently shown that the quality of this relationship is an important contributor to therapeutic outcome (see, for example, Beutler et al., 1994; Horvath and Symonds, 1991; Krupnick et al., 1996; Lambert and Bergin, 1983; Orlinsky and Howard, 1986).

Third, cognitive psychology suggests that expertise has both ordinary and special features (Duncker, 1945). The ordinary part is that *all* human reasoning entails a predictable capacity to carry through a problem-solving cycle: that is, to inspect available data; form a mental model/hypothesis; seek information to test alternative hypotheses; refine the mental model; produce a judgement; seek and inspect confirmatory data, etc. A version of this cycle was proffered by George Kelly in his psychology of personal constructs (Kelly, 1955) in which he argued that all people are automatically scientific in their thought processes.

A question begged, then, is what is special about specialists? Some points have already been noted – the abstract nature of expert cognitive operations compared to those of novices, the discretionary nature and flexibility of expert judgements and actions, and the capacity to articulate a reflexive account of action (summary 'meta-statements'). Hoffman (1998) notes that in some forms of expertise, specialists manifest peculiar perceptual skills. In the case of clinical psychologists this might involve subtle judgements about the salience of non-verbal behaviour in patients. Hoffman also notes that although experts can articulate an overall rationale for their actions, the fine detail of expertise often will be 'unconscious' or 'implicit' or 'tacit' knowledge. In the helping professions such as medicine, social work and the psy complex, case by case comparisons and the use of 'clinical experience' constitute the art (rather than the science) of professional practice. Senior clinicians operate an ordinary and a specialist form of reasoning concurrently in their daily work. They deploy quotidian conversational skills and forms of understanding alongside particular techniques, routines and 'tricks of the trade' learned from their training and supervised work.

However, the cognitive approach has two shortcomings. First, it can only account for the internal workings of expertise (at the individual or micro-social level). It cannot account for why this or that form of expertise has arisen in the way that it has in a particular social context. For example, why in modern societies is a value placed upon stylised forms of conversation directed at the improvement of the well-being of people with personal difficulties? The answer to this resides in a socio-historical investigation outside the frame of reference of cognitive psychology.

Second, in relation to the psy complex (NB not just clinical psychology), knowledge is highly contested and this raises a number of questions. What *exactly* marks out clinical psychology expertise as a special form of knowledge? If it is about increased confidence and credentials in one therapeutic model (say CBT or psychodynamic psychotherapy) how are clinical psychologists different from those in other professions applying the same models? If, on the other hand, it is about the exposure to, and integration of, a broad set of competing knowledge claims in the domain of academic psychology, how do we know that this integration is *actually* delivered by clinical psychologists in their moment-to-moment work? What is the difference between haphazard eclecticism and reflective integration? How do we know that an integrative form of knowledge is better or more efficient than one expressed by a single model of understanding? As several paradigms exist in the psy complex how do we know that the 'meta-paradigm' of clinical psychology's level 3 skills is superior to any one of its constituent parts?

This set of questions does not imply that the actions of clinical psychology are simply forms of bad faith or that professional discourses in the psy complex more generally are mere rhetoric. However, the questions are very challenging for professionals. Some ultimately may be answered empirically. Others may be very difficult or impossible to answer. For example, given that much of the work of the psy complex entails private conversations between a practitioner and a client, how can the minutiae of these exchanges be rendered transparent for the purposes of empirical evaluation and democratic accountability? Whilst these awkward questions do not inevitably imply that the psy complex is not to be trusted by clients and potential clients, they might signal that its practitioners are not *necessarily* to be trusted.

In summary, the criteria for expertise derived from cognitive psychology may be attractive, but they are quickly rendered problematic by professional rhetoric, taking us back to the neo-Weberian and poststructuralist critiques noted above. While the cognitive approach emphasises knowledge and its manifestation in the individual performances of experts, the sociology of the professions raises a number of points about power and the role of middle-class interest groups (like clinical psychology) in society. We now turn to a model derived from the study of organisational behaviour, which might helpfully extend and incorporate both of these aspects.

Power, knowledge and tradeability in psychological expertise

The contributions of sociology and cognitive psychology discussed above imply that an important relationship exists, when understanding expertise, between power and knowledge. Foucauldians, in particular, are preoccupied with this relationship (as a compound notion of 'power/knowledge'). Even those outside this poststructuralist framework acknowledge the importance of knowledge as a source of power. However, there is another aspect to professional life suggested by neo-Weberian sociology. That is, what is the economic viability or market worth of particular forms of expertise?

To be highly knowledgeable in and of itself brings the individual some degree of heightened social status and credibility. But to be sustained as a collective activity, rather than merely exist as personal cleverness, knowledge must be tradeable. Professionals are hired privately by clients and/or are salaried by the state. This distinguishes *professional* expertise from other forms. For example, trainspotters and successful quiz contestants are in their own way experts but they are not professionals. The latter are defined by their collective capacity to sustain an income from their credentialed knowledge. As we noted in Chapter 2, Larson has concluded that 'Professionalization is...an attempt to translate one order of scarce resources – special knowledge and skills – into another – social and economic rewards' (Larson, 1977: xvii).

The precarious distinction between clinical and counselling psychology discussed above implies that it may be tradeability, not knowledge *per se*, which is sometimes crucial. As the older partner, clinical psychology has established training pathways in a number of universities, backed up by NHS funding. By contrast, the capacity of counselling psychologists to compete in the market place with their clinical colleagues is limited by a shorter history, fewer feeder universities and no tradition of NHS-funded training. Moreover, as we highlighted in the quote from the statement issued by the Division of Clinical Psychology (DCP, 2001b: 7), clinical psychologists are keen to mediate (i.e. control) the tradeability of counselling and forensic psychologists.

Fleck (1998) describes the relationship between knowledge, power and tradeability as a 'trialectic' (a conceptual extension of the notion of 'dialectic; see Figure 6.1).

Fleck argues that different academic disciplines focus their attention on each (important) point in this triangular relationship. Thus, epistemological questions, about the formation and nature of knowledge, are addressed by philosophy. Power is the focused concern of sociology. Tradeability is the particular disciplinary interest of economics. Fleck suggests that the interrelationship of the three points in the triangle of expertise requires some form of interdisciplinary understanding. This interdisciplinary work can explore a dynamic relationship which he calls the 'credibility cycle'(see Figure 6.2).

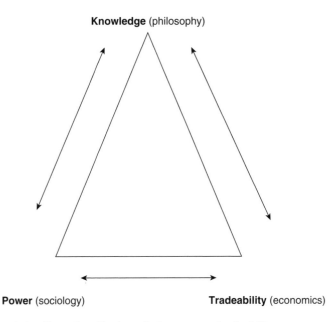

Figure 6.1   *Expertise: the knowledge, power, tradeability trialectic (modified from Fleck, 1998)*

That is, the credibility of particular bids for legitimacy from experts requires competition with others in the market, negotiation with employers, a demonstration of (objective) credentials and the (subjective) persuasion of others concerning practitioner trustworthiness. Moreover, tradeability itself implies that there is an external demand for a service.

Clinical psychology, like other professions, is in the business of defining its knowledge base, sustaining its credibility, extending its political influence and justifying a well-paid occupational niche in society. Since the Second World War, as we noted in Chapter 1, the profession has gone through phases in which these tasks have been approached differently. At first internal epistemological concerns predominated (the knowledge point in the trialectic). During this phase (1950–80) the profession could simply rely on society's faith in science to generate credibility and power. After 1980 power was sought more deliberately, with the beginnings of managerialism in the profession and the push for registration. Given that there were more patients than the mental health services could cope with, the profession did not have to concern itself with the question of external demand.

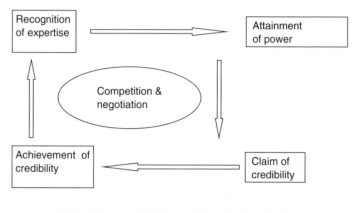

Figure 6.2   *The credibility cycle (modified from Fleck, 1998)*

In the 1990s, however, the profession went through a complex and contradictory phase in relation to both credibility and trade-ability. Its credibility was boosted by the installation of a longer training period with a taught doctorate credential attached. As noted in Chapter 5, the legal mandate under the 1983 Mental Health Act is likely to change and once responsible medical officers (RMOs) are replaced by 'clinical supervisors' (who could be either consultant psychologists or psychiatrists) the gap in status and identity between medicine and clinical psychology will narrow yet further. However, in parallel with these developments, the profession's credibility has also been undermined during the past ten years by some high profile cases of malpractice – mainly in relation to the sexual abuse of patients. These incidents have propelled the BPS into tightening up their procedures for dealing with errant therapists, though these changes did not satisfy some of its members or mental health advocacy groups. (For a fuller discussion of this issue and its implications for professional regulation see Garrett, 1999; Pilgrim and Guinan, 1999; Pilgrim, 2002.)

Meanwhile, the emergence of credible competitors (counselling psychologists, forensic psychologists and nurse therapists) is beginning to impinge on the tradeability of the profession. In response to these pressures the profession has recently sought to extend its influence by involvement in workforce planning. After many years (1979–97) of Conservative attempts to 'quasi-marketise' or 're-commodify' the NHS (the internal market, separation of purchasers and providers, fundholding GPs, etc.) there has been a return to bureaucratic planning. In this post-1997 context, the Division of Clinical Psychology issued a statement with an important opening gambit:

> Psychological care and psychological aspects of health and social care, are at the heart of current national priorities for health services.... The services that clinical psychologists can provide are therefore of huge national importance in the modern NHS, yet the clinical psychology workforce remains inadequate as it has been for decades. (DCP, 2002 SDSC Leaflet 6:1)

As we saw in Chapter 3, the profession has recently been successful in persuading government to address this issue. However, by the time that numbers in the profession expand because of recent increases in the training places being funded by the NHS, the relationship of supply and demand may go into reverse. Instead of a weak supply of newly qualified practitioners leading to their ready employment, the expanding role of others in the psy complex (some of whom are cheaper to employ) may lead to job scarcity in the profession.

Conclusion

This chapter has extended explorations earlier in the book relating to the knowledge base of the profession. It has used frameworks from sociology and cognitive psychology to account for the claims clinical psychology has made for its specific form of expertise. By examining the concept of expertise, we can illuminate some of the contradictions of the profession. Its knowledge base may be complex but its uniqueness, ironically, may only reside in this complexity. The individual components of the latter are not the monopoly of clinical psychology or, for that matter, any other profession in the psy complex. This is true whether we think of particular therapeutic models, such as CBT, or of particular functions, such as assessment and research. Clinical psychologists are costly to employ compared to other mental health workers deploying similar interventions, though not as expensive as medical psychotherapists in the NHS.

The implication of these characteristics of the profession is that it is by no means self-evident that it should, or will, continue to exist as a form of expertise in modern society. Also, assumptions that psychological interventions are benign and 'user-friendly' compared to a biomedical approach to treatment have now been undermined in academic circles by postmodern critiques, while recent publicity about abusive therapists has tarnished the image of all the health professions, including clinical psychology.

Despite these threats to the sustainability of the profession, a bid has been made for expert legitimacy, which may keep it afloat and even extend its influence, relates to clinical health psychology (see the quote from the SDSC leaflet above). The profession may successfully persuade the Department of Health that 'psychological care and psychological aspects of health and social care', which are enjoying the status of a health policy priority in the NHS generally, should be the sole managerial responsibility of clinical psychology.

Finally, in mental health and intellectual disability services, the imminent introduction of the Clinical Supervisor role (in England and Wales) may rescue clinical psychology from the uncertainties noted by these challenges to its credibility and tradeability. As psychiatry discovered long before clinical psychology, a professional knowledge base may be derided or criticised, and the daily role performed by clinicians may be distrusted, but the legal mandate and duty to exercise a version of social control usually ensure the high market value of an occupational group.

7

INTERNAL AND EXTERNAL RELATIONSHIPS

This final chapter will take stock of British clinical psychology by examining both its internal and external relationships. The first of these refers to the inner workings of the profession – to what extent is the profession divided philosophically and segmented organisationally? Or, taking the inverse of these questions, to what extent, as a group of health care workers, is the profession coherent and cohesive? The second set of relationships is about the interface of the profession with colleagues in other professions, the NHS and the State. In other words, what is the character of the boundary between the profession and the wider social system that situates, shapes and constrains its activity? Because this chapter pulls threads in the book together, we will refer back to earlier chapters where appropriate and underline their headline messages.

Internal relationships

There are a number of ways in which clinical psychologists relate to one another that reflect ideological factions and segmented working arrangements. At times they act in unison by enabling their representatives in the Division of Clinical Psychology to present one public voice, even if there are differences of opinion behind the scenes. A good example of this is the public position taken by DCP representatives with the Department of Health about the incipient Mental Health Act reform in England and Wales, despite divergent views among its members (see Chapter 5).

The reason for the lack of unity in the profession partly reflects disparate and contradictory historical threads (see Chapter 1). Even within the first few years of professionalisation, at the Institute of Psychiatry during the 1950s, Hans Eysenck was involved in a volte-face about the role of the profession – eschewing psychological therapy in 1950 and then, in 1958 endorsing it. Thereafter, the split between behaviour therapists at the Institute and psychodynamic psychotherapists at the Tavistock Clinic festered and arguably remains unhealed. Over the years this schism has extended beyond these institutions and has been played out in innumerable scenarios. For example, when clinical psychologists produced a report in 1990 about psychological approaches to psychosis, psychodynamic therapists expressed their anger that the therapeutic bias of the report was towards cognitive-behaviour therapy (Bolsover, 2001; Kinderman, 2001).

Although the managerialism of the 1980s suppressed these tensions about therapeutic ideology for a while, they resurfaced in the 1990s and were exacerbated by postmodernist trends in the social sciences, which were influencing some of the newer recruits. The core orthodoxy in clinical psychology concerning the scientist-practitioner role is predicated upon a major current of Anglo-American empiricism, which is derived from a mixture of experimentalism, methodological behaviourism and psychometrics. However, this core rhetoric of justification about applied science does not neatly or authentically reflect the values and methodological preferences of all psychologists. For example it does not represent the position of either psychodynamic or postmodern psychology. This being the case, the profession inevitably remains fragmented in relation to the question of what should or should not constitute a form of human science (see Chapter 2). Thus, it is their status as applied human scientists that makes clinical psychologists particularly prone to fractious factionalism and internecine disputes.

Apart from the contested epistemological foundations of the profession, clinical psychologists are also divided by speciality and sub-speciality. Unlike the first set of divisions, this one is characterised less by dispute and more by ignorance. For example, clinical psychologists working in intellectual disability services might share more of a common understanding about their daily work with nurses in the same service, than they would with colleagues in the same profession who work in a different speciality. This point is even more pertinent where services are highly specialised: for example, delivering less commonly available therapeutic approaches, such as dialectical behaviour therapy, or working in a sub-speciality such as spinal injury rehabilitation. In some instances, boundaries between specialities are becoming formalised. For example, clinical neuropsychologists have recently formed a discrete camp, with the establishment of a Division of Neuropsychology whose members will be required to complete additional post-qualification training. Similarly, the BPS Register of Psychotherapists which is currently being introduced will produce another enclave within the profession that will define itself through possession of specialist skills (BPS, 2002b). This segmentation is the result of the profession operating in an increasingly complex organisational framework – health care organisations are complex and can only function by differentiation and specialisation. The point applies to all health care professions, not just clinical psychology, and reflects the external context rather than the internal motives of the profession.

A final internal division is that between the clinic and the academy. As noted in Chapter 2, academic clinical psychologists produce most of the research and publications on behalf of the profession. In this sense, clinical psychology almost consists of two separate cultures, with a clear split between research and practice. However, academic departments also run training courses and are highly reliant on NHS colleagues for support as teachers and supervisors for trainee clinical psychologists. In turn, clinical departments depend on the training courses for the production of new recruits. So the two cultures that co-exist within the profession are mutually reliant. Shapiro (2002) suggests that, in future, both camps will benefit from increased collaboration and offers the model of the Psychological Therapies Institute at the University of Leeds, where research is conducted by teams of clinical academics and NHS psychologists on one-day-per-week secondments.

Now that we have summarised some of the internal relationships that characterise the profession, we will move on to consider the interface between the profession and its external context.

External relationships

In the following sections, we will examine the relationship between the profession and the organisations (particularly the NHS) and individuals (both other professionals and service users) who are external to it. In daily practice these interfacing relationships are rarely separate and discrete; instead they coexist, and ebb and flow in their salience to practitioners.

The NHS

British clinical psychology has been in existence for the same period of time as the National Health Service. This has given it some peculiar characteristics. Whereas the older and larger professions, such as medicine and nursing, were well established by 1948 and thus engaged with the new structure in ways that reflected their pre-existing tribal interests, clinical psychology barely existed until the early 1950s. Given its small numbers, the profession was politically marginal for many years. Indeed, its internal concerns about its function (disinterested science vs. therapy) and then the debates about therapeutic ideology (the tension between behaviour therapy and psychodynamic psychotherapy) preoccupied the energy of the profession for over twenty years. In 1977 the Trethowan Report (see Chapter 1) marked the point when a declaration of independence required the profession to define itself with reference to others, especially medicine.

The Trethowan Report largely reflected disaffection in the profession about medical dominance, and the outcome of the report set the scene for a different set of political priorities. Once the green light was given for the profession to become independent and organise itself managerially in localities within the NHS, *managerialism* began to resonate in the profession. This was then strongly reinforced by a shift of power from clinicians to managers in the NHS as a whole, with the introduction of new management arrangements during the mid-1980s.

Apart from managerialism, the question of its *knowledge base* has always been relevant in defining the profession's culture and character. For the first twenty years, the emphasis on British empiricism (especially the methodological behaviourism associated with the psychology department of the Institute of Psychiatry) was very evident and the profession had the reputation of being populated exclusively by behaviour therapists. This reputation or stereotype was strengthened by the decline of the Tavistock Clinic training course, which removed a psychodynamic counterbalance to the behaviourist reputation of the profession.

These epistemological tensions in the profession were submerged, in the main, by the managerialism of the 1980s. However, they did not disappear altogether. Their reappearance in the 1990s was reinforced by another organisational priority for the NHS, the *evidence-based practice* (EBP) movement, which came to the fore because of political preoccupations with cost-minimisation and cost-effectiveness (see Chapter 5).

In this post-Trethowan context, the adaptation of behaviourism to inner life, driven by influential psychiatrists like Aaron Beck in the USA and Isaac Marks in Britain, came as a sharp reminder that psychiatry was still relevant to the workings of clinical psychology. The recent hegemony of cognitive-behaviour therapy (CBT, which sometimes is narrowly, if inaccurately, conflated with 'cognitive therapy') fits well with EBP. It is possible to operationalise this intervention and test its efficacy in randomised controlled trials. Other therapeutic approaches have been tested out less well in this regard and some are less readily evaluated.

One of the outcomes of cognitive-behaviour therapy's dominant position in the armature of clinical psychology is that this has arguably reinforced the medical model, since the evidence base for CBT has developed in relation to diagnostic-related groups (DRGs; see, for example, Department of Health, 2001a). DRGs create a contradiction for the profession, as they are not formulations of particular problems but *a priori* categories, into which patients' presenting symptoms are fitted. This is at odds with a different tradition in the profession of unique psychological formulations. That tradition contains not just those of a more biographical therapeutic persuasion (humanistic and psychodynamic psychotherapists) but also those within experimental psychology, typified in the 1950s by the work of Monte Shapiro and the functional analysis tradition of radical behaviourists. An indication of the unresolved tension that is created for the profession by CBT being applied to DRGs in the NHS, is that some CBT therapists have returned to an emphasis on a psychological approach to formulation, begun by Vic Meyer and developed by Stanley Rachman, to oppose the legitimation of psychiatric categories (Bruch and Bond, 1998).

Another, more recent consequence of the NHS being the principal organisational context for the work of clinical psychologists is that the resource constraints of a state-funded monopoly health care supplier have produced pressures and constraints within the profession. It is now common for NHS psychology services to struggle with chronically long waiting lists and waiting times. This has had a number of consequences.

- It has created stress and demoralisation in NHS practitioners.
- It has necessarily led to creativity in developing briefer and circumscribed interventions, rather than open-ended therapeutic relationships.
- The scarcity of clinical psychologists in a context of high demand led to the proposal by the MPAG in 1988 of a shift from therapy to consultancy, although at the time of writing, this still remains an under-developed professionalisation strategy.
- The recognition that there were inadequate numbers in the profession led to a long period of political lobbying by the DCP to increase training places (see Chapter 3). This lobby has been successful and training courses have grown in number and size over the past ten years – expanding from 19 courses offering 207 places in 1990 to 24 courses providing 454 places in 2001.
- Psychology services have become more professionally varied, with budgets being used to employ staff who are not clinical psychologists.

- The dearth of clinical psychologists has led to a recurrent encroachment of other staff on the therapeutic terrain of clinical psychology, just as clinical psychologists had earlier encroached on the territory of psychiatrists (see Chapter 6). Where this has resulted in lower labour costs, the prospect arises of newly trained people finding it difficult to find work, particularly given the recent increase in training places. This seems paradoxical, given that there has been a training bottleneck in the profession for so long, but there are already signs of this trend in some areas.
- In some localities (mainly large cities) clinical psychology's inability to meet the demand for its services has created the economic opportunity, or necessity, for private practitioners to absorb an overflow of richer clients unwilling to wait for an NHS appointment. Some of these therapists are clinical psychologists, while others are professional rivals.

Central government

The profession's relationship with the state is largely synonymous with its relationship with its employer: the NHS. However, the government departments which now oversee the NHS in Britain are subject to different devolved arrangements in England, Wales and Scotland. For this reason, there are different policies in these three countries, which at times affect clinical psychologists differentially. One common issue that the Westminster government has recently taken very seriously has implications for the whole profession: professional regulation. At the time of writing, the government is introducing legislation to regulate standards in all the health professions – driven by a series of high profile scandals like the one involving children's cardiac services at Bristol Royal Infirmary. New legislation will introduce directives about training, supervision and continued professional development as well as greater protection of patients from neglect or mistreatment. The latter has a particular pertinence for clinical psychologists because of the criticisms directed at the British Psychological Society, about abusive practitioners in its midst (Pilgrim and Guinan, 1999; Pilgrim, 2002: see Chapter 6).

One of the major regulatory frameworks that has recently been introduced into the NHS is the Health Professions Council (HPC), which was established by the Health Professions Order 2001 and replaces the Council for Professions Supplementary to Medicine. The HPC was set up in April 2002 and currently regulates 12 health professions: art, music and drama therapists, chiropodists and podiatrists, clinical scientists, dietitians, medical laboratory technicians, occupational therapists, orthoptists, prosthetists and orthotists, paramedics, physiotherapists, radiographers and speech and language therapists. The BPS is currently pursuing membership of the HPC and hopes to come under this umbrella by late 2004.

In Chapter 1 we noted that the DCP rejected the recommendation of the Seighart Report (1978) for registration of psychotherapists, but campaigned for state registration of psychologists. The BPS Register of Chartered Psychologists was authorised by the Privy Council in 1987, but so far registration has remained voluntary. The Society's preference has always been for a regulatory body specific to psychology, like the General Medical Council for medical practitioners, but the government has made it clear that this is not an option. Faced with the other alternatives – the HPC or a new body to regulate psychotherapy, counselling and psychology – the BPS opted to pursue membership of the HPC. Registration will become compulsory once the profession joins the HPC, when it will become formally committed to accreditation and continuing professional development (see Chapter 4). The HPC may also eventually approve training standards and disciplinary matters, and handle complaints against members of the profession.

The BPS is also continuing to pursue registration of psychotherapists within the profession. Earlier attempts to regulate the practice of psychotherapy in Britain led to the establishment of the United Kingdom Council of Psychotherapy (UKCP) as a credential-awarding body. However, divisions between different branches of psychotherapy resulted in splinter groups establishing their own registers. Thus, clinical psychologists who completed post-qualification training in psychodynamic therapy were able to seek registration with the Confederation of British Psychotherapists, while the vast majority of clinical psychologists (who practise cognitive-behaviour therapy) could pursue registration with the Behavioural and Cognitive Psychotherapy Section of the UKCP, or the British Association of Behavioural and Cognitive Psychotherapies (BABCP).While these options for voluntary registration of psychotherapists remain, the BPS is currently in the process of establishing its own Register of Psychologists as Psychotherapists, although membership remains voluntary at present.

In England and Wales other imminent changes to mental health law will have implications for the profession if enacted, particularly if 'clinical supervisors' replace responsible medical officers (see Chapter 5). Decisions about legal detention and case management under mental health law, previously under the jurisdiction of psychiatry, will be devolved in some cases to psychologists (although it is likely that these cases will be restricted to those involving patients with a diagnosis of personality disorder). When this happens psychologists will face novel practical, ethical and political challenges.

In addition to the government's interest in the political agenda of dangerousness and mental health, it has also announced a national service framework (NSF) of standard setting for mental health in England and Wales (DoH, 1999a). This was the first of a series of national service frameworks that have now been produced and it referred only to people of working age (separate NSFs for children and older people were age defined and generic: i.e. they were not specifically about mental health). The mental health NSF listed seven standards covering mental health promotion; primary care and access to services (two standards); effective services for people with a diagnosis of severe mental illness (two standards); 'carers' of those with mental health problems; and suicide reduction. Whilst clinical psychologists potentially could be involved in delivering or researching all of these seven standards, the four in the middle (referring to primary care and specialist mental health services) have the greatest relevance to the clinical psychology workforce. More specifically, standard two states that:

> Any service user who contacts their primary health care team with a common mental health problem should: • have their mental health needs identified and assessed • be offered effective treatments, including referral specialist services for further assessment, treatment and care if they require it. (DoH, 1999a: 28)

Given the problem noted earlier about demand outstripping supply of psychological therapists, the first word in this standard ('Any') is highly significant. It implies that psychological therapy services cannot operate exclusion criteria. Moreover, under this condition, if services are to deliver rapid access and achieve short or no waiting lists then there are enormous resource implications for the NHS. Service commissioners who have government-devolved budgets (for now these are called Primary Care Trusts) have many competing demands on their resources.

At the time of writing, it is becoming clear that a tension exists between government expectations (prescribed in documents like NSFs) and the ability of the state at local level (represented by organisations like the Primary Care Trusts) to pay for these expectations. In other words, central government demands a certain level of service quality and volume throughout the country but it does not necessarily guarantee the resources to meet the specific local expectations encouraged by this central prescription. This gap between policy prescription and financial capacity has recently brought the NHS as a whole into political crisis and, for some, disrepute.

Other professionals

We noted above that working in the same part of a clinical service means that clinical psychologists may share a common understanding with colleagues in other professions. However, there is another aspect to this shared context: it can be a site of rivalry and antagonism. In the field of adult mental health, this was most obvious during the 1970s in relation to the hostilities that developed in most localities between clinical psychologists and psychiatrists. Much of the time this problem was resolved by clinical psychologists leaving psychiatric services and working in primary care. In other service arenas tensions have been less evident between clinical psychologists and medical practitioners. For example, because they are not fighting a battle for dominance of a particular client group, clinical psychologists in primary care and physical medicine generally enjoy non-conflictual relationships with medical colleagues.

More recently, the shift towards psychological therapy services recruiting a range of therapists has led to tensions as these workers threaten to encroach on the therapeutic territory of clinical psychologists. These other groups include counselling psychologists, nurse therapists and other psychological therapists, from a variety of disciplinary backgrounds, employed on *ad hoc* grades.

Service users

A recent report from Mike Wang, the Chair of the DCP (Wang, 2003), acknowledges that the medical Royal Colleges and other professional bodies are well ahead of the DCP and BPS in facilitating user involvement in their bureaucratic processes. This generally starts with the establishment of patient liaison groups, which may then seek representation on other committees and the opportunity to comment on policies. Wang advocates the establishment of a user liaison group for the DCP to start closing this gap. At the time of writing it is difficult to appraise the overall position that clinical psychology takes about service users because the latter have different characteristics in different clinical arenas. For example, in primary care a user perspective on mental health problems is much more difficult to obtain than in secondary care. In the first arena, clients generally expect anonymity and do not see themselves as part of a collective patient group, whereas in the second it is now common for psychiatric patients in most localities to offer their views of service quality.

In the field of intellectual disability, the question of user involvement in services has been influenced more than in other specialities by the 'normalisation' movement developed by Wolfensberger and Glenn (1975). This movement emphasises the civil rights of people with intellectual disabilities and the ways in which others are involved in their social exclusion. It is commonplace in such services for psychologists to go beyond patient-centredness and to move into the politics of social inclusion (Leyin, 2001). In older people's services it is carer rather than user involvement that tends to assume the higher profile because of the challenges of dementia, although patients' views have sometimes been sought by clinical psychologists.[1]

Because *ipso facto* their approach is psychological, clinical psychologists broadly adopt a patient-centred approach in their interactions, whichever therapeutic model they favour. Thus, at the level of individual casework they could justify a user-centred approach to their work as a routine aspect of their *modus operandi*. However, this is by no means unambiguous, as we saw in Chapters 4 and 5. For example, those working in secure services or with acute psychiatric patients detained under civil sections of the Mental Health Act are arguably part of an apparatus of social control, with third party interests operating (such as those of the criminal justice system, patients' relatives, and the general public). The debate we noted in the profession about plans under new mental health legislation to use clinical psychologists as 'clinical supervisors' highlights the gap between those *already* involved in this social control role (particularly working in forensic settings) and the wider prospect of the role for other psychologists.

The literature produced by British clinical psychologists in the last ten years about user involvement has mainly (but not exclusively) referred to secondary adult mental health care. These publications can be divided into work concerned with enabling user involvement (Holmes, 1996; Jeffery et al., 1997; Newnes and Shalan, 1998; Pilgrim and Waldron, 1998); user involvement in staff recruitment (Long et al., 2000); user views of specific parts of mental health services (Arscott et al., 1997; Goodwin et al., 1999; Toone et al., 1999) and user views on questionnaire completion in service audit exercises (Elscombe and Westbrook, 1996).

Outside the adult mental health field, there have also been reports on consultation exercises with older people in the early stages of dementia (Boakes and Smyth, 1995) and with learning disability service users (Jenkins and Grey, 1994; Thornton, 1997; Waddell and Evers, 2000). It is also now increasingly common for clinical psychology training courses to include learning slots for trainees on user and carer involvement and for trainees to conduct small-scale research on this when on clinical placement.

Self-help and popular psychology

Since the supply for helping relationships often outstrips demand in modern society and given the problems of stigma, time and personal embarrassment attached to help-seeking, some people prefer self-help for their problems in living. Self-help groups (as distinct from bibliotherapy) can be an adjunct to therapy, offer an alternative to therapy, or even shade into self-advocacy. The latter has had a particular relevance in the field of mental health because of the growth in a new social movement of psychiatric patients opposed to professional orthodoxy in mental health services (Rogers and Pilgrim, 1991). Moreover, the growth in the mental health service users' movement has included self-help initiatives surrounding specific symptoms (e.g. the Hearing Voices Network) as well as the development of user-provided clinical services (Pilgrim and Rogers, 2001). Self-advocacy groups (such as People First) have also emerged in the field of intellectual disabilities – an approach which has coalesced with the ideology of normalisation promoted by many clinical psychologists working in that field.

Some clinical psychologists assert that excessive consumer demand mainly warrants more professional resources. Others generate popular self-help texts (for example Rowe, 1983; Fennell, 1999; Butler, 1999; Kennerley, 2000) – as do psychiatrists (for example Peck, 1990; Persaud, 1998; Scott, 2001) and therapists from different backgrounds (for example Fontana, 1989). However, the majority of clinical psychologists take an intermediate position – seeing self-help as an adjunct to therapy that can be cost-effective and easily accessible.

In the USA, where there is a greater cultural reliance on various forms of psychological therapy than in Britain, it is commonplace for therapists to suggest self-help reading for clients. Reviewing this North American picture, Pantalon (1998) notes the following:

- Meta-analyses of self-help material suggest that it is an effective adjunct to therapy, though there is less evidence available about its effectiveness without concurrent or prompting professional contact.
- A majority of therapists (between 55 per cent and 88 per cent) suggest such material to clients during their work.

- Therapists vary in their views about self-help material. Some condemn it as offering misleading false promises to readers (e.g. Rosen, 1987) whereas many therapists, from a variety of therapeutic stables, endorse its use and make a point of spending time writing material for the lay reader.
- The type, length and complexity of the material are highly variable. It includes therapy manuals (with CBT-based approaches being particularly common); general self-help books; material that is either problem-specific or technique-specific; Internet material (from information to online therapy); and educational self-help books. The last of these focus on providing information about the patients' problems in order to encourage a collaborative response from patients and their significant others.

Leaving aside the question of effectiveness, it is worth considering the function of self-help material. Its very existence, and the large market associated with it, imply that a large chunk of society has been induced into believing in the wisdom of psychological expertise – what de Swaan (1990) has called a process of 'protoprofessionalisation'. The material is cheaper than private psychotherapy and more readily available than therapy provided by the state. It may also be less embarrassing or threatening for a client to engage with a book or a computer than a person. Furthermore, those who have had negative or abusive experiences at the hands of professional therapists may understandably feel safer with bibliotherapy. In one respect this is justified (paper cannot abuse but therapists can and do), although individual risk/distress may be increased by inappropriate/ineffective treatment – whether this is delivered by a person or a book.

The evolution of self-help material mirrors, in part, the change in discourse about psychotropic medication. The latter started (prior to the 1950s) with an emphasis on symptom relief, primarily by sedation. Later (after 1960) the emphasis was curative and antipsychotics, antidepressants and anxiolytics were introduced. In the last twenty years, the claims for medication have extended to giving people *without* significant mental health problems enhanced functioning, mood or quality of life. Similarly, the self-help material available covers symptom reduction, offers of major existential change for those already distressed and promises of greater fulfilment for those who are not seeking help from mental health professionals. Thus, self-help material entails its recipients casting themselves in the role of patient, whether or not they also occupy this role formally in relation to a service or therapist.

In conclusion, self-help material is based upon a mixture of therapeutic approaches (see Glossary), some of which reflect a current professional orthodoxy. The literature outside this orthodoxy includes spiritual texts, just as it did in the first half of the century (see Chapter 1). However, what all of the material has in common is some version of the 'good life'– a view of which forms of conduct and states of being are deemed to be worthy and which are not. In this regard the literature is no different from the models of therapy it reflects, except that in the latter the notion of what constitutes the 'good life' is often less explicit.

Continuing debates in clinical psychology

The profession faces many challenges including pressure to deliver training to larger numbers of recruits in a more flexible way; the need to develop its consultancy role beyond mere rhetoric; and the demands of an increasingly diverse role that is likely to range from detention of individuals under the new Mental Health Act to growing collaboration with users in the design and delivery of services. In addition to these challenges, the profession continues to define and defend its knowledge base and, of course, this process is shaped by external forces.

Kennedy and Llewelyn (2001) studied the views of trainees, trainers and NHS staff about the needed components of training courses and the political and educational factors shaping them in the future. They concluded that the evidence-based scientist-practitioner model, with critical analytic skills and research competence, may be expected to remain the focus of training (in line with national and international developments in cost-effective, evidence-based health care), while anticipating an increased need for training to mirror NHS priorities. The authors acknowledge that clinical psychologists working in the NHS are faced with two major obstacles when attempting to work as scientist-practitioners: (1) healthcare is dominated by medicine, with its different epistemological base, and (2) the NHS does not adequately fund research or allow its staff sufficient time to carry it out. They suggest that the way forward will involve differing approaches to the scientist-practitioner model: for example, implementation and evaluation of research findings from academic colleagues, and greater emphasis on practice-based research with a willingness to reformulate the model to reflect a more complex view of science than mere positivism (Corrie and Callahan, 2000).

Another continuing debate within the profession concerns the centrality of the biopsychosocial model in both conceptualisation of cases and decisions regarding intervention. Slade (2002) argues that the widespread adoption of this model by psychiatry should not blind us to the fact that mental health teams generally understand emotional disorders primarily in biological terms, with the psychological and social factors receiving consideration only when biological factors fail to account for all phenomena. Slade contends that clinical psychologists have a duty to challenge biological explanations of human distress that have a weak evidence base and have a further duty to undertake research to extend the relevant evidence base. In particular, he suggests that research needs to take account of public preference. A recent survey of over 2,000 members of the British public found that 91 per cent of respondents thought people with depression should be offered counselling while only 16 per cent thought they should be offered medication (Priest et al., 1996). A paternalistic view of this response assumes that the public merely requires better education about 'the optimal use of treatment services' (Jorm et al., 2000). However, Slade's own view differs substantially: in an increasingly consumerist society, he argues, it is surely going to become ever more difficult to justify spending taxpayers' money on forms of treatment they do not want. He therefore advocates a shift away from cost-effectiveness research – concerned with a predetermined (i.e. defined by professionals) set of desirable outcomes – towards cost-utility research that takes service users' preferences and priorities into account.

Gilbert (2002a, 2002b) also finds the biopsychosocial approach to mental health inadequate as it stands, but argues that this is due to a widespread misinterpretation of the model by both doctors and other clinicians. In fact, Gilbert suggests, the biopsychosocial model *is* ideally suited to cope with the growing complexity of the clinical sciences, and he urges clinical psychologists to be at the forefront of efforts to develop this approach to conceptualisation of disorders and their interventions. He concludes that

> we are fooling ourselves if we believe that having more psychologists doing more individual therapies will make much impact on the epidemics of anxiety and depression....Abuse, deprivation and lack of support are the breeding grounds for mental ill-health....A key task is how we can take our biopsychosocial understandings and translate them into a genuine community-based psychology that does not at the same time lose sight of individual suffering and physiological processes. (Gilbert, 2002b: 31)

While Gilbert urges us to look beyond the constraints of individual therapy addressing individual problems, other clinical psychologists are considering yet wider horizons. The recent growth of the Positive Psychology movement in the United States (for example, Seligman and Csikszentmihalyi, 2000) attests to dissatisfaction among an increasing number of clinical psychologists with the exclusive focus on pathology, disorder and distress that has dominated the work of the profession's members. Positive Psychology, which aims to promote subjective well-being, positive personal traits (e.g. interpersonal effectiveness, self-determination) and positive institutions/communities (based on values such as responsibility, tolerance and nurturance), has its antecedents in the humanism of psychologists such as Abraham Maslow and Carl Rogers. Recent proponents of the model do not claim that this is a new perspective, but argue that the influence of its earlier versions was limited by the absence of a sound empirical base and an emphasis on the self that, at times, conflicted with concerns about collective well-being. Seligman and Csikszentmihalyi (2000) make a persuasive case for clinical psychologists to use their scientific skills to create, understand, and measure the factors that allow individuals, communities and societies to flourish. They observe that prevention of human distress requires an approach that enables individuals and communities to systematically build competencies, not one that merely corrects weaknesses.

Conway and MacLeod (2002) offer a British perspective on clinical psychology's neglect of well-being, noting that *The Core Purpose and Philosophy of the Profession* (DCP, 2001b: 2) states that 'Clinical psychology aims to reduce psychological distress and to enhance and promote psychological well-being'. They contend that the profession has focused more or less exclusively on the former – partly because its limited resources have encouraged a reactive approach to the presentation of individual distress, and partly because of an implicit belief that well-being is simply the absence of distress. Conway and MacLeod argue for the existence of well-being as a separate dimension from distress and conclude that there is now substantial evidence that (1) positive aspects of experience are related to protection and recovery from depression, and (2) therapeutic approaches that focus on promoting well-being and quality of life are effective (MacLeod and Moore, 2000). Thus, they join with Seligman and Csikszentmihalyi in encouraging clinical psychologists to research, evaluate and promote well-being in their clients as a means of enhancing good mental health.

These are, then, some of the current debates about the way that the theory and practice of clinical psychologists may develop over the next few decades. The ideas summarised in this section broaden the perspective found in much of the evidence-based psychological treatment literature, with its traditional orientation towards individual pathology, and offer the profession a way forward that is not constrained by an illness model.

Conclusions

This book has brought together a number of threads of understanding that we consider crucial for any reader new to the profession to understand. *History* is important in two senses. First, clinical psychology as the largest applied wing of the academic discipline of psychology has been shaped by its inherited knowledge base. Because this knowledge base is fragmented and contested, those tensions are reflected in the character of the profession. Second, clinical psychology has a relatively short history *as a profession*. Indeed in Britain it has effectively only existed for just over fifty years. Consequently, the peculiarities of British culture after the Second World War have also shaped its character. Within this context, the NHS as the dominant employer of clinical psychologists has to be recognised as a powerful determinant or constraint on the profession.

The profession is also characterised by a series of dynamically interweaving *internal and external relationships*. We cannot answer a general question such as 'What is clinical psychology?' without examining both these internal dynamics and the ways in which the profession interfaces with others.

Third, we have identified the importance of *role ambiguity* in understanding the nature of clinical psychology. Whilst there is a broad agreement that the profession has core functions (assessment, therapy, consultancy, training and research) the way these functions are interpreted and the balance between them is variable in the work of practitioners. This makes it impossible to respond unambiguously to the question 'What is a clinical psychologist?' The ambiguity extends beyond the individual to the variety of service contexts that employ clinical psychologists. For example, varying levels of security in mental health services bring their own constraints and opportunities that shape the way practitioners work with clients. Thus, a clinical psychologist would necessarily work differently in a primary care setting than in a maximum security hospital.

Political ambiguity is also apparent in our account of the profession. Much that we have presented here suggests that clinical psychology, like other professions, is self-serving and therefore preoccupied with social closure and boundary maintenance. At the same time, there are individuals and groups in the profession who are actively fostering collaborative relationships with other social groups and stakeholders and spend little time promoting the collective interests of their profession. There are those who seek multi-disciplinary co-operation and synergy to maximise the efficiency of the service system they inhabit, while others emphasise user involvement and community development initiatives. Even the variegated knowledge base of the profession reflects different political value positions. Some clinical psychologists are committed to a conservative pro-medical and positivist or naïve realist view of the world. This may extend to forms of biological reductionism and genetic determinism. At the other extreme are psychologists who are radical environmentalists or radical constructivists and who seek illumination in their work by studying social and economic relationships. These contrasting views and positions between them shape the political features of particular roles inhabited or advocated by individual clinical psychologists.

The ambiguities, tensions and even conflicts that have characterised the internal and external relationships of British clinical psychology have contributed to its vulnerability at various times, as well as its vigour. A certain amount of cohesion is undoubtedly necessary if a profession is to survive, but we contend that the segmented nature of clinical psychology – ideologically and organisationally – is both inevitable within large health care bureaucracies like the NHS, and essential if we are to respond flexibly and usefully to the wide range of needs we encounter.

Note

1 General conceptual questions surrounding the notions of 'users' and 'carers' and 'user involvement' are discussed in Pilgrim and Rogers (2001).

GLOSSARY OF THERAPEUTIC APPROACHES

This glossary provides very brief accounts of therapeutic approaches used by British clinical psychologists. One key reference is provided with each entry, for optional further reading. Cross-references are shown in bold type. The glossary only alludes to the therapeutic aspect of the role of clinical psychologists. It does not contain entries related to their other professional activities discussed in the book, such as assessment, consultancy and research.

Because therapeutic approaches are not practised only by clinical psychologists, it is important to note that the entries describe activities carried out at times by other professions. For some of these professionals (e.g. psychiatrists, mental health nurses, social workers and occupational therapists) psychological therapies exist on the margins of their practice, and thus they generally deploy them less than clinical psychologists. However, for other professionals (e.g. medical psychotherapists, nurse therapists, counselling psychologists and counsellors) psychological therapy has a more dominant role than it does for some clinical psychologists.

The glossary does not provide an exhaustive list of therapeutic approaches (there are hundreds of them). It is limited to the ones which, in the view of the authors, are most likely to be practised currently by British clinical psychologists. All entries apart from the first one are in alphabetical order.

PSYCHOTHERAPY is a generic term to describe any systematic approach to helping using a form of conversation (also called 'psychological therapy'). Each of the various models described in this glossary then characterises a particular type. Psychotherapy can be used in groups and with families – it is not only about individual casework. The term 'counselling' is more often used in non-health settings but, in practice, the two terms are effectively interchangeable as descriptions of a form of psychological practice or enabling conversation. However, some psychotherapists depict 'counselling' as a less sophisticated or complex process and some counsellors reject the term 'psychotherapy' because of its medical connotations. Another term, which is sometimes used generically, is 'talking treatment'. Broadly speaking, the psychotherapies exist on a continuum.

This ranges from a fluid exploration of the client's biography (such as **person-centred therapy** and **existential therapy**), in which the therapist responds to what the client brings, moment to moment, to more structured and technique-driven approaches (such as **behaviour therapy** and **cognitive-behavioural therapy**). Hence, some psychotherapies are largely exploratory, non-directive and emphasise insight and meaning, whereas others are more structured, prescriptive and emphasise behaviour change. Several therapeutic approaches can be situated in between (such as **personal construct therapy**). Moreover, even action-orientated therapies like cognitive behaviour therapy entail the client revising the meaning of their actions. All models share some other common features, such as an emphasis on a positive working relationship between client and therapist, the importance of good listening and empathy skills on the part of the therapist and, most obviously, the role of talk in engendering personal change. [Feltham, C. (ed.) (1997) *Which Psychotherapy? Leading Exponents Explain their Differences.* London: Sage]

BEHAVIOUR MODIFICATION AND BEHAVIOUR THERAPY. Behaviour therapy emerged in the 1950s with an emphasis on the role of Pavlovian conditioning in generating and maintaining neurotic symptoms. Behaviour modification was based more on operant or Skinnerian conditioning. However, in the clinical literature the two terms are sometimes used interchangeably. Strictly speaking, behaviour modification is used to describe a variety of interventions that aim to decrease the frequency of dysfunctional or maladaptive behaviour, using negative reinforcement or (less commonly) punishment, and shape up more adaptive behaviour using positive reinforcement. Definitions of behaviour therapy vary and include any behavioural techniques that reduce psychological distress. Joseph Wolpe and Hans Eysenck at first emphasised techniques that would reduce anxiety-based symptoms, using knowledge from Pavlovian psychology and learning theory. During the 1970s, behaviour therapists began to work more with inner events (thoughts and feelings) as well as action. Once this occurred, the term was increasingly superseded, first by that of 'cognitive-behaviour therapy' and latterly by that of **cognitive-behavioural therapy.** With this change of technical emphasis came a shift towards the treatment of depression and personality problems, not just anxiety states. [Margraf, J. (1998) Behavioral approaches. In A.S. Bellack and M.Hersen (eds) *Comprehensive Clinical Psychology Volume 6.* Oxford: Pergamon]

COGNITIVE-ANALYTIC THERAPY (CAT), a form of eclectic psychotherapy, was developed by Anthony Ryle in the 1980s and integrated ideas from **personal construct therapy** and **psychoanalysis.** The therapist and client build up a shared formulation of the latter's life and jointly examine the dysfunctional patterns which repeat over time. CAT emphasises both intrapsychic and interpersonal processes. [A. Ryle (ed.) (1995) *Cognitive-Analytic Therapy: Developments in Theory and Practice.* Chichester: Wiley]

COGNITIVE-BEHAVIOURAL THERAPY (CBT) is the most commonly used term to describe the extension of **behaviour therapy** to include interventions targeting thoughts and feelings, as well as behaviours. Sometimes the term 'cognitive behaviour therapy' is used instead. CBT places the emphasis on clients resolving their presenting problems by developing better coping strategies in their lives and modifying the ways in which their beliefs generate and maintain dysfunctional behaviour. The approach is collaborative and clients are encouraged to engage in behavioural experiments between sessions to test out fears and predictions. This emphasis on 'homework' can be found in other models such as **solution-focused brief therapy** but it is absent from interpretive therapies (**psychodynamic psychotherapy)** and exploratory therapies (e.g. **person-centred therapy**). CBT is probably the commonest form of intervention used by clinical psychologists in mental health settings. [Hawton, K., Salkovskis, P.M., Kirk, J. and Clarke, D.M. (1989) *Cognitive Behaviour Therapy for Psychiatric Problems.* Oxford: Oxford Medical Publications]

COGNITIVE THERAPY is a generic term covering a range of therapies that focus on the client's thoughts, feelings and beliefs. Sometimes (somewhat confusingly) it is used as a synonym for **cognitive-behavioural therapy** in the everyday discourse of clinicians. However, more accurately, other prominent cognitive therapies are subsumed by the term, including **cognitive-analytic therapy, rational emotive behaviour therapy** and **personal construct therapy**. [Blackburn, I-M. (1998) Cognitive therapy. In A.S. Bellack and M. Hersen (eds) *Comprehensive Clinical Psychology Volume 6.* Oxford: Pergamon]

DIALECTICAL BEHAVIOUR THERAPY (DBT) is a particular application of **cognitive behavioural therapy** that was developed by Marsha Linehan in the 1980s to assist people with a diagnosis of borderline personality disorder – individuals who often have a history of childhood abuse/neglect. This adaptation of CBT places an additional emphasis on the interpersonal processes involved in helping patients change. The attention to the therapeutic relationship and interpersonal processes in DBT is similar to the emphasis within **interpersonal psychotherapy**. [Linehan, M.M. (1993) *Cognitive-Behavioral Treatment of Borderline Personality Disorder*. New York: Guilford Press]

EXISTENTIAL THERAPY shares similar assumptions with **personal construct therapy** and **person-centred-therapy** about human responsibility and agency. In this model, psychological disturbance is not understood in terms of past conditioning or historical causes. Instead, the emphasis is on the client facing life's challenges in a truthful or authentic way. Existential therapy makes no suppositions about symptoms, other than that they have particular relevance and meaning within a person's biography. The role of the existential therapist is to enable the client to face life authentically using a combination of empathic clarifications and honest challenges. [van Deurzen, E. (2000) Existential counselling and therapy. In C. Feltham and I. Horton (eds) *Handbook of Counselling and Psychotherapy*. London: Sage]

INTERPERSONAL PSYCHOTHERAPY (IPT) has evolved over the past thirty years from an approach originally developed by Gerald Klerman and Myrna Weissman in the context of a North American clinical trial evaluating treatment of depression. IPT also derives from the work of Harry Stack Sullivan and Adolf Meyer and assumes that the onset, response to treatment and outcome in depression are influenced by the interpersonal relations of the depressed individual with significant others. Clients are assisted in making links between their current low mood and specific interpersonal events that are maintaining their difficulties. Therapy thus takes an interpersonal rather than an intrapsychic focus and concentrates on assisting the depressed person to utilise available social support more effectively and, where appropriate, to develop their existing social network. IPT is a time-limited intervention with a collaborative and descriptive emphasis similar to that of **cognitive-analytic therapy**. It has now been developed for application to a wide range of psychological disorders. [Klerman, G.L., Weissman, M.M., Rounsaville, B.J. and Chevron, E.S. (1984) *Interpersonal Psychotherapy of Depression*. New York: Basic Books]

PERSON-CENTRED THERAPY derives from the work of Carl Rogers in the 1950s and is also called 'client-centred counselling'.

Rogers was committed to the idea that the resources for personal change were inherent in clients and that it was the role of the therapist, via the therapeutic relationship, to offer support and facilitation for this potential in human growth. For this reason, Rogers did not emphasise technique but the therapist's personal qualities – they should be genuine, warm and empathic. He considered these to be the necessary and *sufficient* conditions for psychological change. [Merry, T. (2000) Person centred counselling and therapy. In C. Feltham and I. Horton (eds) *Handbook of Counselling and Psychotherapy*. London: Sage]

PERSONAL CONSTRUCT THERAPY (PCT) is derived from the work of George Kelly in the 1950s, who emphasised the unique ways in which individuals construe their world. When a person's personal construct system becomes dysfunctional or distressing they are encouraged to work collaboratively with the PCT therapist, who flexibly combines empathy with challenge and experimentation to help the client re-construe their world to their advantage. Constructivist approaches have been developed further in psychotherapy especially by family therapists under the influence of postmodern social science. PCT was one important source of **cognitive-analytic therapy**, although its role in this has lessened. PCT remains a form of therapy in its own right. [Fransella, F. and Dalton, P. (1996) Personal construct therapy. In W. Dryden (ed.) *Individual Therapy in Britain*. London: Sage]

PSYCHOANALYSIS is a broad term which refers to the work of Sigmund Freud, and to that of his followers who adhered to his views or modified them whilst retaining the term. The emphasis in psychoanalysis is on the therapist making interpretations of the client's life and their flow of verbalisations within the therapeutic relationship. The model (whatever its variations) emphasises unconscious mental life and its role in generating neurotic or dysfunctional activity. The analyst interprets this unconscious material, making very sparse interventions during sessions, and does not advise or direct the client, although the client is encouraged to simply say whatever is on their mind ('free association'). In its pure form psychoanalysis is very intensive (five times per week for many years). However, it is shortened and diluted within **psychodynamic psychotherapy.** [See the comparative section on 'Psychodynamic approaches' therapy in C. Feltham and I. Horton (eds) *Handbook of Counselling and Psychotherapy*. London: Sage]

PSYCHODYNAMIC PSYCHOTHERAPY is a term used to describe any form of psychotherapy derived from psychoanalysis or from the works of those who split away from Freud (such as Carl Jung and Alfred Adler) or later modified his views (such as Melanie Klein, Ronald Fairbairn, Donald Winnicott and John Bowlby). It is sometimes called 'psychoanalytical psychotherapy' or simply 'dynamic psychotherapy'. Whatever the name used, the approach always emphasises unconscious mental life and the role of interpretation by the therapist in encouraging insight in the client. Whereas **psychoanalysis** is primarily concerned with understanding the unconscious, forms of dynamic psychotherapy, as well as being less intensive in frequency, focus more on personal change. [See the comparative section on 'Psychodynamic approaches' therapy in C. Feltham and I. Horton (eds) *Handbook of Counselling and Psychotherapy*. London: Sage]

RATIONAL EMOTIVE BEHAVIOUR THERAPY (REBT) was developed by Albert Ellis in the 1950s (and at that time was called 'rational therapy'). Ellis changed the name to 'rational emotive therapy (RET)' in 1962 and altered it again in 1993 to 'rational emotive behaviour therapy', although in Britain the term RET is still often used. The focus of this approach is on challenging the client's irrational beliefs about themselves and the world. The goal of therapy is to enable the client to shift towards a clearer and less rigid way of thinking, which will bring with it reduced distress and greater fulfilment in life. This 'thinking' emphasis places RET firmly within the domain of **cognitive therapy**. [Dryden, W. (1996) Rational emotive behaviour therapy. In W. Dryden (ed.) *Handbook of Individual Therapy*. London: Sage]

SOLUTION-FOCUSED BRIEF THERAPY (SFBT) Whereas most models of therapy focus on uncovering, understanding and working with the client's problems, SFBT for the great part avoids 'problem talk'. Instead it focuses on the client's preferred future and how far they have already moved towards achieving it. This entails drawing attention to what has already been achieved, what next steps could be taken and what exceptions there are to the problem in their life (i.e. when the problem is not there). The 'brief' aspect to the approach does not necessarily signify duration of time, but refers to the minimum number of sessions needed for the client to become autonomous of therapy. As in **cognitive-behavioural therapy,** there is an emphasis on inter-sessional experimentation by clients to try out new solutions. However, this is framed less as prescribed 'homework' and more as optional work for the client to consider. [Hawkes, D., Marsh, T. and Wigosh, R. (1998) *Solution Focused Therapy: A Handbook for Healthcare Professionals.* Oxford: Butterworth/Heinemann]

FURTHER READING

Bunn, G.C., Lovie, A.D. and Richards, G.D. (2001) *Psychology in Britain*. Leicester: BPS Books.

Carr, A. (1999) *The Handbook of Child and Adolescent Clinical Psychology: A Contextual Approach*. London: Routledge.

Emerson, E., Hatton, C., Bromley, J. and Caine, A. (eds) (1998) *Clinical Psychology and People with Intellectual Disabilities*. Chichester: Wiley.

Jones, D. and Elcock, J. (2001) *History and Theories of Psychology*. London: Arnold.

Leahey, T.H. (2001) *A History of Modern Psychology*. Third edition. Upper Saddle River, NJ: Prentice Hall.

Marzillier, J. and Hall, J. (eds) (1999) *What is Clinical Psychology?* Third edition. Oxford: Oxford University Press.

APPENDIX

The British Psychological Society can be contacted at:

St Andrews House
48 Princess Road East
Leicester LEI 7DR

Tel 0116 254 9568
Fax 0116 247 0787

www.bps.org.uk   Information requests: enquiry@bps.org.uk

Further information on clinical psychology training and how to apply is available from:

The Clearing House for Postgraduate Courses in Clinical Psychology
15 Hyde Terrace
Leeds LS2 9LT

chpccp@ leeds.ac.uk
www.leeds.ac.uk/chpccp

The Affiliates Group of the Division of Clinical Psychology of the British Psychological Society represents the interests of assistant and trainee clinical psychologists. Officers of the Committee of the Affiliates Group can be contacted through the BPS for information about assistant psychology posts or clinical psychology training. The Affiliates Group also produces a *Handbook* containing information on the training courses provided by current trainees. The *Alternative Handbook* can be obtained from the BPS.

REFERENCES

Abbott, A. (1988) *The System of the Professions*. London: University of Chicago Press.

Agnew, S., Carson, J. and Dankert, A. (1995) The research productivity of clinical psychologists and psychiatrists: a comparative study. *Clinical Psychology Forum*, 86: 2–5.

Armstrong, D. (1980) Madness and coping. *Sociology of Health and Illness*, 2 (3): 393–413.

Arscott, K., Bollom, P., Dawson, O. and King, M. (1997) User views of two psychiatric day centres. *Clinical Psychology Forum*, 102: 34–39.

Atkinson, P. (1981) *The Clinical Experience: The Construction and Reconstruction of Medical Reality*. Farnborough: Gower.

Bannister, D. and Fransella, F. (1970) *Inquiring Man*. Harmondsworth: Penguin.

Baty, F.J. (1998) A clinical psychology service for older adults – the integrated primary care model. *PSIGE (Psychologists Special Interest Group Working with Older People) Newsletter*, 67: 3–6.

Baty, F., Blakey, R., McPherson, F. and Peaker, A. (2001) What has GP fund holding taught us? *Clinical Psychology*, 5: 16–18.

Bergin, A.E. and Garfield, S.L. (eds) (1994) *Handbook of Psychotherapy and Behavior Change*. Fourth edition. New York: John Wiley & Sons.

Beutler, L.E., Machado, P.P. and Neufeldt, S.A. (1994) Therapist variables. In A.E. Bergin and S.L. Garfield (eds) *Handbook of Psychotherapy and Behavior Change*. Fourth edition. New York: John Wiley & Sons.

Black, T. (2001) The new Mental Health Act. Letter to *Clinical Psychology*, 7: 3–4.

Boakes, J. and Smyth, C. (1995) Finding out from older people. *Clinical Psychology Forum*, 83: 6–8.

Boddington, S. (2001) National Service Framework for Older People: summary and thoughts from a clinical psychologist's perspective. *PSIGE (Psychologists Special Interest Group Working with Older People) Newsletter*, 77: 5–11.

Bolsover, N. (2001) Science and fiction (letter). *Clinical Psychology*, 5: 5–6.

Bostock, J. (1998) From clinic to community: generating social validity in clinical psychology. *Clinical Psychology Forum*, 121: 2–5.

Bourke, J. (2001) Psychology at war. In G.C. Bunn, A.D. Lovie and G.D. Richards (eds) *Psychology in Britain*. Leicester: BPS Books.

Boyle, F.M.L., Lindsay, W.R. and McPherson, F.M. (1997) A primary care-based clinical psychology service. *Clinical Psychology Forum*, 106: 22–24.

Bridgeman, P.W. (1927) *The Logic of Modern Physics*. New York: Macmillan.

British Psychological Society (1998) *Code of Conduct*. Leicester: BPS, July.

British Psychological Society (2001a) *The Royal Charter, the Statutes, the Rules*. Leicester: BPS.

British Psychological Society (2001b) Division of Clinical Psychology's *Guidelines for Continuing Professional Development*. Leicester: BPS.

British Psychological Society (2001c) Division of Clinical Psychology's Special Interest Group in Children and Young People: Position Paper. *Guidelines for Commissioning and Purchasing Child Clinical Psychology Services*. Leicester: BPS.

British Psychological Society (2002a) *Clinical Psychology Services for Older People in Primary Care*. Division of Clinical Psychology Occasional Paper No. 4. Leicester: BPS.

British Psychological Society (2002b) Society. *The Psychologist*, 15 (5): 258.

Bucher, R. and Stelling, J. (1977) *Becoming Professional*. London: Sage.

Bucher, R., Stelling, J. and Dommermuth, P. (1969) Differential prior socialization: a comparison of four professional training programmes. *Social Forces*, 48: 213–223.

Burton, M. and Adcock, C. (1998) The associate psychologist: developing the graduate psychologist workforce. *Clinical Psychology Forum*, 121: 7–12.

Butler, G. (1999) *Overcoming Social Anxiety and Shyness*. London: Constable & Robinson.

Carchedi, G. (1977) *On the Economic Identification of the New Middle Class*. London: Routledge & Kegan Paul.

Carr, A. (1999) *The Handbook of Child and Adolescent Clinical Psychology: A Contextual Approach*. London: Routledge.

Castel, F., Castel, R. and Lovell, A. (1979) *The Psychiatric Society*. New York: Columbia Free Press.

Cattrall, R., Carney, P., Collins, S., Cox, R., Dunn, C., Hawkins, C., Holmes, G., Jones, H., Maclachlan, A., McQueen, C., Newnes, C., Owens, M., Perrin, A. and Pitts, C. (2001) Clinical psychologists and the new Mental Health Act. Letter to *Clinical Psychology*, 5: 7–8.

Cheshire, K.E. (2000) Professional socialisation in clinical psychology trainees. Unpublished PhD thesis. University of Liverpool.

Clare, A. (1979) Review of *Psychiatry Observed* by G. Baruch and A. Treacher, *Psychological Medicine*, 9: 387–389.

Claridge, G.S. and Brooks, D.N. (1973) A survey of applicants for the Glasgow MSc course in clinical psychology: some applications for selection and training. *Bulletin of the British Psychological Society*, 26: 123–127.

Clearing House for Postgraduate Courses in Clinical Psychology: Handbook for 2002 Entry (2002) University of Leeds.

Clinical Psychology Forum (1999) Special Issue: Evidence-Based Practice. 133 (November).

Code, L. (1991) *What Can She Know? Feminist Theory and the Construction of Knowledge*. Ithaca, NY: Cornell University Press.

Collins, S. and Murray, A. (1995) A pilot project employing counselling psychologists within an adult mental health clinical psychology service. *Clinical Psychology Forum*, 78: 8–12.

Conway, C. and MacLeod, A. (2002) Well-being: its importance in clinical practice and research. *Clinical Psychology*, 16: 26–29.

Cooke, A., Harper, D. and Kinderman, P. (2001) DCP update. Reform of the Mental Health Act: implications for clinical psychologists. *Clinical Psychology*, 1: 48–52.

Cooke, A., Harper, D. and Kinderman, P. (2002) 'DCP update. Do clinical psychologists care about the Mental Health Act reforms?' *Clinical Psychology*, 15: 40–46.

Cooke, A., Kinderman, P. and Harper, D. (2002) DCP update: Criticisms and concerns. *Clinical Psychology*, 13: 43–47.

Copeland, J., Davidson, I., Dewy, M., Gilmore, C., Larkin, B., McWilliam, C., Saunders, P., Scott, A., Sharman, V. and Sullivan, C. (1992) Alzheimer's disease, other dementias, depression and pseudo-dementia: prevalence, incidence and three-year outcome in Liverpool. *British Journal of Psychiatry*, 161: 230–239.

Corrie, S. and Callahan, M. (2000) A review of the scientist-practitioner model. *British Journal of Medical Psychology*, 73: 413–427.

Cox, K. (1995) Clinical practice is not applied scientific method. *Australia and New Zealand Journal of Surgery*, 65: 553–557.

Crawford, D. (1989) The future of clinical psychology: whither or wither? *Clinical Psychology Forum*, 20: 29–31.

Crawford, M. (2000) Homicide is impossible to predict. *Psychiatric Bulletin*, 24: 152.

Crompton, R. (1987) Gender, status and professionalism. *Sociology*, 21: 413–428.

Cupitt, C. (2001) Developing psychology posts in assertive outreach. *Clinical Psychology*, 5: 48–50.

Cushway, D. (1992) Stress in clinical psychology trainees. *British Journal of Clinical Psychology*, 31: 169–179.

Dadds, M.R. (1995) *Families, Children, and the Development of Dysfunction*. London: Sage.

Danziger, K. (1997) *Naming the Mind: How Psychology Found its Language*. London: Sage.

Davies, C. (1996) The sociology of professions and the profession of gender. *Sociology*, 30 (4): 661–678.

Day, C. and Wren, B. (1994) Journey to the centre of primary care: primary care psychology in perspective. *Clinical Psychology Forum*, 65: 3–6.

de Swaan, A. (1990) *The Management of Normality*. London: Routledge.

Department of Health (1997) *The New NHS: Modern, Dependable*. London: HMSO.

Department of Health (1998) *A First Class Service: Quality in the NHS*. London: DoH.

Department of Health (1999a) *The National Service Framework for Mental Health*. London: HMSO.

Department of Health (1999b) *Drug Misuse and Dependence – Guidelines on Clinical Management*. London: HMSO.

Department of Health (2001a) *Treatment Choice in Psychological Therapies and Counselling: Evidence-Based Clinical Practice Guidelines*. London: DoH.

Department of Health (2001b) *Mental Health National Service Framework (and the NHS Plan): Workforce Planning, Education and Training*. Final Report by the Workforce Action Team, August. London: DoH.

Department of Health (2001c) *National Service Framework for Older People*. London: DoH.

Department of Health (2002) *Delivering the NHS Plan: Executive Summary*. Norwich: HMSO.

Department of Health and Home Office (2000) *Reforming the Mental Health Act*. London: HMSO.

Department of Health and Social Security (1977) *The Role of Psychologists in the Health Service*. London: HMSO.

Derksen, M. (2001) Science in the clinic: clinical psychology at the Maudsley. In G.C. Bunn, A.D. Lovie and G.D. Richards (eds) *Psychology in Britain*. Leicester: BPS Books, pp. 267–289.

Dewey, J. (1886) *Psychology*. New York: Holt.

Diamond, B. (2001) Reform of the Mental Health Act: social cohesion or coercion? *Clinical Psychology*, 4: 8–9.

Division of Clinical Psychology (1998) *Guidelines for the Employment of Assistant Psychologists*. Leicester: BPS.

Division of Clinical Psychology (2001a) *Guidelines for CPD*. Leicester: BPS.

Division of Clinical Psychology (2001b) *The Core Purpose and Philosophy of the Profession*. Leicester: BPS.

Division of Clinical Psychology (DCP) (2002) Guidance on clinical workforce planning. *SDSC*, leaflet 6:1.

Division of Counselling Psychology (2001) *Statement of Professional Aims*. Leicester: British Psychological Society.

Dobson, K.S. and Craig, K.D. (eds) (1998) *Empirically Supported Therapies: Best Practice in Professional Psychology*. London: Sage.

Dreyfus, H.L. and Dreyfus, S.E. (1986) *Mind Over Machine*. New York: Free Press.

Duncker, K. (1945) On problem solving. *Psychological Monographs*, 58: 1–113 (Trans. L.S. Lees).

Edelmann, R.J. (2001) Decline in applications for clinical psychology training. Letter to *Clinical Psychology*, 4: 5–7.

Edgell, B. (1961) The British Psychological Society 1901–41. Special supplement of the *Bulletin of the British Psychological Society*.

Elscombe, S. and Westbrook, D. (1996) How do adult users of psychology services feel about filling in questionnaires? *Clinical Psychology Forum*, 96: 11–15.

Eysenck, H.J. (1949) Training in clinical psychology: an English point of view. *American Psychologist*, 4: 173–176.

Eysenck, H.J. (1950) Function and training of the clinical psychologist. *Journal of Mental Science*, 96, 710–725.

Eysenck, H.J. (1952) *The Scientific Study of Personality*. London: Routledge & Kegan Paul.

Eysenck, H.J. (1953) *Uses and Abuses of Psychology*. Harmondsworth: Penguin.

Eysenck, H.J. (1958) The psychiatric treatment of neurosis. Paper presented to the Royal Medico-Psychological Association, London.

Fennell, M. (1999) *Overcoming Low Self-Esteem*. London: Constable & Robinson.

Fleck, J. (1998) Expertise: knowledge, power and tradeability. In R. Williams, W. Faulkner and J. Fleck (eds) *Exploring Expertise: Issues and Perspectives*. Basingstoke: Macmillan.

Fontana, D. (1989) *Managing Stress*. London: British Psychological Society and Routledge.

Foster, J. (1971) *Enquiry into the Practice and Effects of Scientology*. London: HMSO.

Fothergill, R. (2000) Primary healthcare nurses and mental health problems affecting older adults: development and evaluation of a training package. *PSIGE (Psychologists Special Interest Group Working with Older People) Newsletter*, 72: 21–24.

Foucault, M. (1965) *Madness and Civilisation*. New York: Random House.

Foucault, M. (1973) *The Order of Things: An Archeology of the Human Sciences*. New York: Vintage Books.

Frankish, P. (1999) The role and future of community psychology. *Clinical Psychology Forum*, 124: 28–30.

Freidson, E. (1970) *The Profession of Medicine: A Study of the Sociology of Applied Knowledge*. New York: Harper & Row.

Fryer, D. (1998) Community psychology: practising what we (don't) teach? *Clinical Psychology Forum*, 122: 45–47.

Gallagher, H. and Brosnan, N. (2001) Evaluating the supervision experiences of assistant psychologists. *Clinical Psychology*, 8: 39–42.

Gambril, E. (1990) *Critical Thinking in Clinical Practice*. San Francisco: Jossey-Bass.

Garrett, T. (1999) Sexual contact between clinical psychologists and service users: a response to Pilgrim. *Clinical Psychology Forum*, 132: 13–14.

Gellner, E. (1988) *Plough, Sword and Book*. London: Collins Harvill.

Gieryn, T. (1999) *Cultural Boundaries of Science: Credibility on the Line*. Chicago: University of Chicago Press.

Gilbert, P. (2002a) Understanding the biopsychosocial approach: I. Conceptualization. *Clinical Psychology*, 14: 13–17.

Gilbert, P. (2002b) Understanding the biopsychosocial approach: II. Individual and social interventions. *Clinical Psychology*, 15: 28–32.

Gold, A. (2000) Involving significant others in pain management programmes: a survey of current practice in the UK. *Clinical Psychology Forum*, 138: 26–30.

Goldberg, D. and Huxley, P. (1992) *Common Mental Disorders: A Biosocial Model.* London: Routledge.

Goodwin, A. (2001) Uses and misuses of clinical psychology in the mental health rehabilitation system. *Clinical Psychology*, 1: 37–41.

Goodwin, I., Holmes, G., Newnes, C. and Waltho, D. (1999) A qualitative analysis of the views of inpatient mental health service users. *Journal of Mental Health*, 8 (1): 43–54.

Gray, I. (2001) Training numbers in England 2001–4. *Clinical Psychology*, 2: 47.

Green, B. (1994) Developing a primary care and community psychology service. *Clinical Psychology Forum*, 65: 32–35.

Hall, J. (1997) Counsellors and psychologists: a subjective experience of working together. *Clinical Psychology Forum*, 101: 18–21.

Hall, J. and Firth-Cozens, J. (2000) *Clinical Governance in the NHS: a Briefing.* Division of Clinical Psychology Information Leaflet No.4. Leicester: BPS.

Hallam, A.M. (1925) The threshold of practical psychology. *Practical Psychologist*, 1: 1.

Hallam, R.S., Bender, M. and Wood, R. (1989) Letter to *The Psychologist*, 2 (9): 375.

Halliday, T.C. (1983) Professions, class and capitalism. *Archives Européens de Sociologie*, 24: 321–346.

Halliday, T.C. (1987) *Beyond Monopoly.* London: University of Chicago Press.

Handy, J. (1991) Stress and contradiction in psychiatric nursing. *Human Relations*, 44 (1): 39–53.

Harper, D. (1990) Assistant psychologists and supervision. *Clinical Psychology Forum*, 26: 33–36.

Harper, D. and Newton, T. (1988) Psychology technicians: their use and abuse. *Clinical Psychology Forum*, 17: 5–10.

Hayes, S.C. (1998) Scientific practice guidelines in a political, economic, and professional context. In K.S. Dobson and K.D. Craig (eds) *Empirically Supported Therapies: Best Practice in Professional Psychology.* London: Sage.

Head, D. and Harmon, G. (1991) The scientist-practitioner in practice: a short reply. *Clinical Psychology Forum*, 33: 33.

Health Psychology AGM (2000) *Minutes of Health Psychology AGM.* Leicester: British Psychological Society.

Hearnshaw, L.S. (1964) *A Short History of British Psychology.* London: Methuen.

Heller, M.B. (1997) Clinical psychologists and counsellors: working together in an agency setting. *Clinical Psychology Forum*, 101: 13–17.

Hetherington, R. (1981) The changing role of the clinical psychologist. *Bulletin of the British Psychological Society*, 34: 12–14.

Hoffman, R.R. (1998) How can expertise be defined? Implications of research from cognitive psychology. In R. Williams, W. Faulkner and J. Fleck (eds) *Exploring Expertise: Issues and Perspectives.* Basingstoke: Macmillan.

Holmes, G. (1996) Bringing about change in a psychiatric hospital: the Patients' Council at Shelton two years on. *Clinical Psychology Forum*, 95: 25–28.

Holmes, G. (2002) Some thoughts on why clinical psychologists should not have formal powers under the new Mental Health Act. DCP Update. *Clinical Psychology*, 12: 40–43.

Horvath, A.O. and Symonds, B.D. (1991) Relation between working alliance and outcome in psychotherapy: a meta-analysis. *Journal of Counselling Psychology*, 38: 139–149.

Hoshmand, L.T. and Polkinghorne, D.E. (1992) Redefining the science–practice relationship and professional training. *American Psychologist*, 47 (1): 55–66.

Jacox, A. (1973) Professional socialization of nurses. *Journal of New York State Nurse Association*, 4 (4): 6–15.

James, W. (1890) *Principles of Psychology*. 2 vols. New York: Dover Books.

Jamous, H. and Peloille, B. (1970) Changes in the French university hospital system. In J.A. Jackson (ed.) *Professions and Professionalization*. Cambridge: Cambridge University Press.

Jefferis, P., Volans, J. and Minter, M. (1997) A survey of research activities, skills and training needs in a clinical psychology department. *Clinical Psychology Forum*, 108: 13–14.

Jeffery, D., Burrows, M. and West, J. (1997) Do we really want to know? Barriers to service users' expression of their views and some ways of overcoming them. *Clinical Psychology Forum*, 102: 9–14.

Jenkins, J. and Grey, L. (1994) Multidisciplinary audit by a service for people with learning disabilities: quality assessment and sampling consumer views. *Clinical Psychology Forum*, 69: 22–29.

Johnson, T. (1979) The professions in the class structure. In R. Case (ed.) *Industrial Society: Class, Cleavage and Control*. London: George Allen & Unwin.

Jones, D. and Elcock, J. (2001) *History and Theories of Psychology*. London: Arnold.

Jones, H.G. (1984) Behaviour therapy – an autobiographic view. *Behavioural Psychotherapy*, 12: 7–16.

Jorm, A.F., Angermeyer, M. and Katschnig, H. (2000) Public knowledge of and attitudes to mental disorders: a limiting factor in the optimal use of treatment services. In G. Andrews and A. Henderson (eds) *Unmet Need in Psychiatry*. Cambridge: Cambridge University Press.

Kahn, R.L., Wolfe, D.M., Quinn, R.P., Snoek, J.D. and Rosenthal, R.A. (1964) *Organizational Stress Studies in Role Conflict and Ambiguity*. New York: John Wiley.

Kat, B. (1994) The contribution of psychological knowledge to primary health care: taking a step back to go forward. *Clinical Psychology Forum*, 65: 23–26.

Kelly, G. (1955) *The Psychology of Personal Constructs*. New York: Norton.

Kemp, E. and Thwaites, R. (1998) A comparison of adult mental health patients allocated to counselling and clinical psychology. *Clinical Psychology Forum*, 121: 13–16.

Kendell, R.E. (2000) The next 25 years. *British Journal of Psychiatry*, 176: 6–9.

Kennedy, P. and Llewelyn, S. (2001) Does the future belong to the scientist practitioner? *The Psychologist*, 14 (2): 74–78.

Kennerley, H. (2000) *Overcoming Childhood Trauma*. London: Constable & Robinson.

Kinderman, P. (2001) The future of clinical psychology training. *Clinical Psychology*, 8: 6–10.

Kinderman, P. (2002) Reforms to the Mental Health Act: a call for action by members. Letter to *Clinical Psychology*, 10: 2–3.

Kiseley, S.R. and Goldberg, D.P. (1996) Physical and psychiatric co-morbidity in general practice. *British Journal of Psychiatry*, 169: 236–242.

Krupnick, L.J., Sotsky, S.M., Simmens, S., Moyer, J., Elkin, I., Watkins, J. and Pilkonis, P.A. (1996) The role of the therapeutic alliance in psychotherapy and pharmacotherapy outcome: findings in the National Institute of Mental Health Treatment of Depression Collaborative Research Programme. *Journal of Consulting and Clinical Psychology*, 64: 532–539.

Lambert, M.J. and Bergin, A.E. (1983) Therapist characteristics and their contribution to psychotherapy outcome. In C.E. Walker (ed.) *The Handbook of Clinical Psychology*, Vol. 1. Homewood, IL: Dow Jones–Irwin, pp. 205–241.

Larson, M.S. (1977) *The Rise of Professionalism: A Sociological Analysis*. London: University of California Press.

Lawton, R. and Parker, D. (1999) Procedures and the professional: the case of the British NHS. *Social Science and Medicine*, 48: 353–361.

Leahey, T.H. (2001) *A History of Modern Psychology*. Third edition. Upper Saddle River, NJ: Prentice Hall.

Lee, T., Critchley-Robbins, S., Smyth, C., McDonagh, C. and Dooley, C. (2002) Implementing the National Service Framework for Older People: what can clinical psychologists do? *PSIGE (Psychologists Special Interest Group Working with Older People) Newsletter*, 79: 17–24.

Leonard, R. and Burns, A. (2000) The paradox of older women's health. In J.M. Ussher (ed.) *Women's Health. Contemporary International Perspectives*. Leicester: BPS.

Levenson, V.L. (2001) The role of clinical supervisor. Letter to *Clinical Psychology*, 3: 3.

Lewin B. et al. (1992) Effects of self-help post-myocardial infarction rehabilitation on psychological adjustment and use of health services. *Lancet*, 339: 1036–1040.

Leyin, A. (2001) The evolution of psychological approaches in working with people with learning disabilities. *Clinical Psychology Forum*, 148: 12–17.

Long, C.G. and Hollin, C.R. (1997) The scientist-practitioner model in clinical psychology: a critique. *Clinical Psychology and Psychotherapy*, 4 (2): 75–83.

Long, N., Newnes, C. and MacLachlan, A. (2000) Involving service users in employing clinical psychologists. *Clinical Psychology Forum*, 138: 39–42.

Lund, C. (2002) Withdrawal from statement of equivalence. Letter to *Clinical Psychology*, 8: 3–5.

McAllister, T.A. and Phillip, A. (1975) The clinical psychologist in a health centre: one year's work. *British Medical Journal*, 4: 513–514.

Macdonald, K.M. (1995) *The Sociology of the Professions*. London: Sage.

McGarry, J., Bhutani, G.E. and Watts, S. (1997) A survey of mental health needs in older adult recipients of Primary Care Services. *PSIGE (Psychologists Special Interest Group Working with Older People) Newsletter*, 59: 19–22.

McGuire, B., Bekker, A., Green, D. and Keogan, C. (2001) The Statement of Equivalence in clinical psychology: problems and prospects. *Clinical Psychology*, 6: 34–35.

MacLeod, A. and Moore, R. (2000) Positive thinking revisited: positive cognitions, well-being and mental health. *Clinical Psychology and Psychotherapy*, 7: 1–10.

McPherson, F.M. (1983) Organization of psychological services. In A. Liddell (ed.) *The Practice of Clinical Psychology in Great Britain*. London: John Wiley & Sons.

McPherson, F. and Baty, F. (2000) The reorganization of primary care in Scotland and the implications for clinical psychology. *Clinical Psychology Forum*, 143: 14–17.

Management Advisory Service (1996) Psychological therapies. *MAS Partnership Bulletin*. Winchcombe: MAS.

Mann, A.H. et al. (1992) The Gospel Oaks Study: the prevalence and incidence of dementia in an inner city area of London. *Neuroepidemiology*, 11 (Supplement 1): 76–79.

Mansell, J., Orford, J., Reicher, S. and Stephenson, G. (1991) Editorial. *Journal of Community and Applied Psychology*, 1: 1–4.

Markman, P. (2002) Further thoughts on the Mental Health Act. Letter in *Clinical Psychology*, 9: 4–5.

Marzillier, J. and Hall, J. (eds) (1999) *What is Clinical Psychology?* Third edition. Oxford: Oxford University Press.

Meddings, S. (1999) Developing assertive outreach services. *Clinical Psychology Forum*, 127: 43–45.

Meddings, S. and Cupitt, C. (2000) Clinical psychologists and assertive outreach: a briefing paper for the Division of Clinical Psychology of the British Psychological Society. *Clinical Psychology Forum*, 137: 47–51.

Medlik, L. (1999) Primary care groups and clinical psychology. *Clinical Psychology Forum*, 131: 9–12.

Meltzer, H., Gatward, R., Goodman, R. and Ford, T. (2000) *The Mental Health of Children and Adolescents in Great Britain*. London: Office of National Statistics.

Menzies, I.E.P. (1977) *The Functioning of Social Systems as a Defence against Anxiety*. Tavistock Pamphlet No.3. London: The Tavistock Institute of Human Relations.

Miller, P. and Rose, N. (eds) (1986) *The Power of Psychiatry*. Cambridge: Polity Press.

Miller, R. (1994) Clinical psychology and counselling in primary care: opening the stable door. *Clinical Psychology Forum*, 65: 11–14.

Miller, R. (1997) Thesis or synthesis: to boldly go where no psychologist and counsellor have gone before. *Clinical Psychology Forum*, 101: 41–43.

Miller, R. and Wilson, J. (1998) 'I could do that!': competence, roles and training in the delivery of psychological healthcare. *Clinical Psychology Forum*, 116: 15–18.

Miller, W.R. and Rollnick, S. (1991) *Motivational Interviewing – Preparing People to Change Addictive Behavior*. New York: Guilford Press.

Milne, D. (1987) Projects: a way of combining research and practice. *Clinical Psychology Forum*, 9: 9–14.

Milne, D. (1999) Editorial: important differences between the 'scientist-practitioner' and the 'evidence-based practitioner'. *Clinical Psychology Forum*, 133: 5–9.

Mollon, P. (1989) Narcissus, Oedipus and the psychologist's fraudulent identity. *Clinical Psychology Forum*, 23: 7–11.

Murphy, G. (1928) *An Historical Introduction to Modern Psychology*. London: Kegan Paul, Trench & Trübner.

Murray, G. and McKenzie, K. (1998) Sex differences and promotion prospects in clinical psychology in Scotland. *Clinical Psychology Forum*, 115: 25–29.

Navarro, V. (1986) *Class Struggle, the State and Medicine*. London: Martin Robertson.

Newnes, C. and Shalan, D. (1998) Fear and loathing in Patients' Council visitors. *Clinical Psychology Forum*, 111: 27–30.

Niebor, R., Moss, D. and Partridge, K. (2000) A great servant but a poor master: a critical look at the rhetoric of evidence-based practice. *Clinical Psychology Forum*, 136: 17–19.

Olesen, V. and Whittaker, E.W. (1968) *The Silent Dialogue*. San Francisco: Jossey-Bass.

Oppenheimer, M. (1975) *The Proletarianisation of the Professional*. *Sociological Review* Monograph No. 20.

Orford, J. (1998) Have we a theory of community psychology? *Clinical Psychology Forum*, 122: 6–10.

Orlinsky, D.E. and Howard, K.I. (1986) Process and outcome in psychotherapy. In S.L. Garfield and A.E. Bergin (eds) *Handbook of Psychotherapy and Behaviour Change*. Third edition. New York: Wiley, pp. 311–384.

Ørner, R.J., Avery, A. and Stoltz, P. (2000) EBP deconstructed and reconstructed. Letter to *Clinical Psychology Forum*, 136: 2–4.

O'Sullivan, K.R. and Dryden, W. (1990) A survey of clinical psychologists in the south-east Thames health region: activities, role and theoretical orientation. *Clinical Psychology Forum*, 29: 21–26.

Pantalon, M.V. (1998) Use of self-help books in the practice of clinical psychology. In A.S. Bellack and M. Hersen (eds) *Comprehensive Clinical Psychology* (Vol. 6). New York: Pergamon.

Papworth, M.A. (2000) Primary care psychology: towards a model of service delivery. *Clinical Psychology Forum*, 142: 22–26.

Parker, I. (ed.) (1999) *Deconstructing Psychotherapy*. London: Sage.

Parry, G. (1989) Care for the future. *The Psychologist*, 2 (6): 436–438.

Patel C. et al. (1985) Trial of relaxation in reducing coronary risk: a four year follow up. *British Medical Journal*, 290: 1103–1106.

Paxton, R. (1987) Why are we here? Some quick and dirty reasons. *Clinical Psychology Forum*, 9: 6–9.

Paxton, R. (2000) Managing psychological therapies departments: what's different? *Clinical Psychology Forum*, 135: 15–18.

Paykel, E.S. and Priest, R.G. (1992) Recognition and management of depression in General Practice: consensus statement. *British Medical Journal*, 305: 1198–1202.

Payne, R.W. (1953) The role of the clinical psychologist at the Institute of Psychiatry. *Revue de Psychologie Appliquée*, 3: 150–160.

Payne, R.W. and Firth, J. (1987) *Stress in Health Professionals*. Chichester: John Wiley & Sons.

Peck, M.S. (1990) *The Road Less Travelled*. London: Arrow Books.

Persaud, R. (1998) *Staying Sane: How to Make Your Mind Work for You*. London: Metro Publishing Ltd.

Pilgrim, D. (1990) Clinical psychology in the 1980s: a sociological analysis. Unpublished MSc thesis, Polytechnic of the South Bank.

Pilgrim, D. (2000) The real problem for postmodernism. *Journal of Family Therapy*, 22 (1): 6–23.

Pilgrim, D. (2002) The emergence of clinical psychology as a profession. In J. Allsop and M. Saks (eds) *Regulating the Health Professions*. London: Sage.

Pilgrim, D. and Guinan, P. (1999) From mitigation to culpability: rethinking the evidence about therapist sexual abuse. *European Journal of Psychotherapy, Counselling and Health*, 2 (2): 153–168.

Pilgrim, D. and Rogers, A. (1999) *A Sociology of Mental Health and Illness*. Second edition. Buckingham: Open University Press.

Pilgrim, D. and Rogers, A. (2001) Users and their advocates. In G. Thornicroft and G. Szmukler (eds) *Textbook of Community Psychiatry*. Oxford: Oxford University Press.

Pilgrim, D. and Treacher, A. (1992) *Clinical Psychology Observed*. London: Tavistock/Routledge.

Pilgrim, D. and Waldron, L. (1998) User involvement in mental health services: how far can it go? *Journal of Mental Health*, 7 (1): 95–104.

Pollert, A. (1996) Gender and class revisited; or, the poverty of 'patriarchy'. *Sociology*, 30 (4): 639–660.

Polyani, K. (1957) *The Great Transformation*. Boston, MA: Beacon Press.

Priest, R.G., Vize, C., Roberts, A., Roberts, M. and Tylee, A. (1996) Lay people's attitudes to treatment of depression: results of opinion poll for Defeat Depression Campaign just before its launch. *British Medical Journal*, 313: 858–859.

Prochaska, J.O., DiClemente, C.C. and Norcross, J.C. (1992) In search of how people change: applications to addictive behaviors. *American Psychologist*, 47 (9): 1102–1114.

Radford, J. and Holdstock, L. (1995) Does psychology need more boy appeal? *The Psychologist*, 8 (1): 21–24.

Raimy, V.C. (ed.) (1953) *Training in Clinical Psychology*. New York: Prentice Hall.

Rappaport, J. (1977) *Community Psychology: Values, Research and Action*. New York: Holt, Rinehart & Wilson.

Reisman, J.M. (1966) *The Development of Clinical Psychology*. New York: Appleton-Century-Crofts.

Rezin, V. and Tucker, C. (1998) The uses and abuses of assistant psychologists: a national survey of caseload and supervision. *Clinical Psychology Forum*, 115: 37–42.

Richards, B. (1983) Clinical psychology, the individual and the state. Unpublished PhD thesis, Polytechnic of North East London.

Rogers, C.R. (1957) The necessary and sufficient conditions for personality change. *Journal of Consulting Psychology*, 21: 95–103.

Rogers, A. and Pilgrim, D. (1991) 'Pulling down churches': accounting for the British mental health users' movement. *Sociology of Health and Illness*, 15 (5): 612–631.

Rogers, A. and Pilgrim, D. (2001) *Mental Health Policy in Britain*. London: Palgrave.

Rose, N. (1985) *Governing the Soul*. London: Routledge.

Rose, N. (1996) *Inventing Our Selves*. Cambridge: Cambridge University Press.

Roth, T. (1999) Evidence-based practice: is there a link between research and practice? *Clinical Psychology Forum*, 133: 37–40.

Rounsaville, B.J., O'Malley, S., Foley, S. and Weissman, M.W. (1988) Role of manual-guided training in the conduct and efficacy of interpersonal psychotherapy for depression. *Journal of Consulting and Clinical Psychology*, 56: 681–688.

Rowe, D. (1983) *Depression: The Way out of Your Prison*. London: Routledge & Kegan Paul.

Ryle, A. (1990) *Cognitive-Analytical Therapy*. London: Wiley.

Sainsbury Centre for Mental Health (1997) *Pulling Together: The Future Roles and Training of Mental Health Staff*. London: Sainsbury Centre for Mental Health.

Sainsbury Centre for Mental Health (1997–8) *Missed Opportunities*. London: Sainsbury Centre for Mental Health.

Saks, M. (1983) Removing the blinkers? A critique of recent contributions to the sociology of the professions. *Sociological Review*, 1: 1–20.

Salmon, T.W. (1917) The care and treatment of mental diseases and war neuroses: 'shell shock' in the British army. *Mental Hygiene*, 1: 509–574.

Saxby, B. and Svanberg, P.O. (1998) *The Added Value of Psychology to Physical Healthcare*. Division of Clinical Psychology Occasional Paper No.2. Leicester: BPS.

Scott, J. (2001) *Overcoming Mood Swings*. London: Constable & Robinson.

Scottish Office Department of Health (1997) *Designed to Care: Renewing the National Health Service in Scotland*. Edinburgh: Scottish Office.

Seighart, P. (1978) *An Investigation into the Practice of Scientology*. London: HMSO.

Seligman, M. (1995) The effectiveness of psychotherapy: the *Consumer Reports* study. *American Psychologist*, 50: 965–974.

Seligman, M. and Csikszentmihalyi, M. (2000) Positive psychology. *American Psychologist*, 55 (1): 5–14.

Shapiro, D. (2002) Renewing the scientist-practitioner model. *The Psychologist*, 15 (5): 232–234.

Shapiro, M. (1951) An experimental approach to diagnostic psychological testing. *Journal of Mental Science*, 97: 747–764.

Shillitoe, R. and Hall, J. (1997) Clinical psychologists and counsellors: working together. *Clinical Psychology Forum*, 101: 5–8.

Simons, H. (1984) *Rhetoric in the Human Sciences*. London: Sage.

Skinner, A. (1996) Research and clinical psychologists. *Clinical Psychology Forum*, 96: 44–45.

Slade, M. (2002) Biopsychosocial psychiatry and clinical psychology. *Clinical Psychology*, 9: 8–12.

Slife, B.D. and Williams, R.N. (1995) *What's Behind the Research: Discovering Hidden Assumptions in the Behavioural Sciences*. London: Sage.

Smail, D. (1982) Clinical psychology – homogenized and sterilized. *Bulletin of the BPS*, 35: 345–346.

Smail, D. (2001) The impossibility of specifying 'good' psychotherapy. *Clinical Psychology*, 7: 14–18.

Smart, B. (1990) On the disorder of things: sociology and the end of the social. *Sociology*, 24 (3): 397–416.

Spellman, D. and Ross, J. (1987) A bridge for the scientist-practitioner gap? *Clinical Psychology Forum*, 11: 19–20.

Spence, M. (1998) Community psychology and the 'mainstream'. *Clinical Psychology Forum*, 122: 14–15.

Stevens, S.S. (1939) Psychology and the science of science. *Psychology/Psychological Bulletin*, 36: 221–263.

Stone, M. (1985) Shellshock and the psychologists. In W.F. Bynum, R. Porter and M. Shepherd (eds) *The Anatomy of Madness*. London: Tavistock.

Thompson, B. (1999) If statistical significance tests are broken/misused, what practices should supplement or replace them? *Theory and Psychology*, 9 (2): 165–181.

Thomson, M. (2001) The popular, the practical and the professional: psychological identities in Britain, 1901–1950. In G.C. Bunn, A.D. Lovie and G.D. Richards (eds) *Psychology in Britain*. Leicester: BPS Books, pp.115–132.

Thornton, P.J. (1997) Consumer evaluation of a challenging behaviour support worker service for people with learning disabilities. *Clinical Psychology Forum*, 102: 3–6.

Toone, H., Reid, D. and Storey, C. (1999) User views of a community drop-in centre for people with mental health problems. *Clinical Psychology Forum*, 132: 22–25.

Ussher, J. (1991) Clinical psychology and sexual equality: a contradiction in terms? *Feminism and Psychology*, 1 (1): 63–68.

Vasco, A.B., Garcia-Marques, L. and Dryden, W. (1993) 'Psychotherapist know thyself': dissonance between metatheoretical and personal values in psychotherapists of different theoretical orientations. *Psychotherapy Research*, 3 (3): 181–196.

Waddell, H. and Evers, C. (2000) Psychological services for people with learning disabilities living in the community. *Clinical Psychology Forum*, 141: 34–38.

Walsh, S. and Cormack, M. (1994) 'Do as we say but not as we do': organizational, professional and personal barriers to the receipt of support at work. *Clinical Psychology and Psychotherapy*, 1 (2): 101–110.

Wang, M. (2003) *What is the DCP Doing? A Report from the Chair*. Leicester: British Psychological Society.

Watts, S.C., Bhutani, G.E., Stout, I.H., Ducker, G.M., Cleator, P.J., McGarry, J. and Day, M. (2002) Mental health in older adult recipients of primary care services: is depression the key issue? Identification, treatment and the general practitioner. *International Journal of Geriatric Psychiatry*, 17 (5): 427–437.

Whittington, A. and Burns, J. (2001) Statement of equivalence developments. Letter to *Clinical Psychology*, 8: 3–4.

Willner, P. and Napier, B. (2001) The statement of equivalence: further problems and a modest proposal. Letter to *Clinical Psychology*, 8: 2–3.

Zadik, T. (1999) EBP: not very NICE. Letter to *Clinical Psychology Forum*, 133: 3.

INDEX

Abbott, A., 26, 29, 36
abstract knowledge, 29
abuse by therapists, 116, 118, 130
Adcock, C., 59–60
Adler, Alfred, 141
Agenda for Change, 65
American Psychological Association,
    14, 37, 86, 94
Assertive Outreach programmes, 72
assistant psychologists, 43–5, 55–6,
    59–60, 75
associate psychologist grade, 59–60
Atkinson, P., 27, 29

Baty, F., 90–3
Beck, A., 21, 122
behaviour therapy, 14, 22, 34–7, 119;
    see also cognitive-behaviour
    therapy
behavioural problems, 69, 74–6
biopsychosocial model, 132
Black, T., 99
Blakey, R., 91
Boulder model, 37
Bowlby, John, 141
Boyle, F.M.L., 92
Bridgeman, P.W., 32–4
Bristol Royal Infirmary, 124
British Association of Behavioural and
    Cognitive Psychotherapists, 125
British Journal of Psychology, 7
British Psycho-Analytical Society, 12
British Psychological Society (BPS),
    5–9, 12, 14, 26, 53–5, 83,
    116, 144
    code of conduct, 60
    Division of Clinical Psychology
        (DCP), 16–18, 51, 58–62,
        67, 87–8, 101, 104–6, 114,
        117, 119, 123–7
    Division of Counselling
        Psychology, 106
    Division of Health Psychology, 77–8
    Division of Neuropsychology, 82, 120
    register of practitioners, 120, 125

Brooks, D.N., 37–8
Brooks, Harry, 9
Brosnan, N., 56
Bucher, R., 49
burn-out, 43, 47, 50
Burt, Cyril, 10, 12–13
Burton, M., 59–60

Carchedi, G., 3
career structure in clinical
    psychology, 59–60, 65
Cattrall, R., 99–100
Cheshire, K., 42, 62
children, services for, 68–70
Claridge, G.S., 37–8
Clearing House for Postgraduate
    Courses in Clinical Psychology,
    52–4, 144
client-centred practice, 109, 139
client groups of clinical psychology,
    68–84
clinical governance, 40, 60–1, 85, 87
clinical neuropsychology, 81–2, 120
Clinical Outcomes Research and
    Effectiveness (CORE), 87
clinical practice, 27–9
clinical protocols, 85–6
clinical psychology
    aims of, 104–5
    characteristics of, 40, 47, 103
    definition of, 5
    factionalism in, 119–21
    history of, 6–19
    as a profession, 19–20, 26,
        39–41, 47, 51, 115, 134
    as a science, 36
    uniqueness of, 117
Clinical Psychology (journal), 99
Clinical Psychology Forum, 86
clinical supervision
    of compulsorily-detained mental
        patients, 98–101, 116, 118,
        125, 128
    of trainee psychotherapists,
        44, 48–50

clinical training, 45–9
Code, L., 108
code of conduct for clinical
    psychology, 60
cognitive-analytic therapy (CAT),
    21–2, 138, 140
cognitive-behaviour therapy (CBT),
    14, 20–1, 107, 120–5, 130, 137–8
cognitive psychology, 21, 110–13, 141
Committee for the Scrutiny of
    Individual Clinical Qualifications,
    54, 57
Committee on Training in Clinical
    Psychology, 53, 58
community psychiatric nurses, 39,
    55, 71
community psychology, 93–7, 100
compulsory treatment of mental
    patients, 98–101
Confederation of British
    Psychotherapists, 125
continuing professional development,
    61–2, 125
Conway, C., 133
*Core Purpose and Philosophy of the
    [clinical psychology] Profession*
    (DCP, 2001), 104–5, 133
Cormack, M., 49–50
cost-effectiveness and cost-utility
    research, 132
Coué, Emile, 9
counselling, 92, 105–6, 114, 136, 139
couple therapy, 67
Cox, K., 27–8
credentialisation, 88
credibility, 114–18
Crichton Royal Hospital,
    Dumfries, 13–14
criminal justice system, 83
Csikszentmihalyi, M., 133

Danziger, K., 34
Davies, C., 4, 6
de Swaan, A., 130
dementia, 73, 128
depression, 73, 81, 132–3, 137, 139
detention of mental patients,
    98–101, 128
Dewey, John, 8
diagnostic-related groups
    (DRGs), 123
dialectical behaviour therapy, 138–9

diametics, 15
Diamond, B., 99
differential psychology, 7
doctoral studies, 45, 51–2, 55–6, 60
Dreyfus, H.L. and S.E., 28
Dryden, W., 38
Durkheim, Emile, 2
dynamic psychotherapy, *see*
    psychodynamic therapy

eclecticism in clinical psychology, 14
effectiveness as distinct from
    efficacy, 67–8
Elcock, J., 11, 33–5, 40
Ellis, Albert, 21, 141
empiricism, 20–2, 107, 120, 122
eugenics, 7, 13, 21
evidence-based practice, 40, 50, 67,
    85–9, 106, 108, 122, 131
Exeter University, 95
existential therapy, 137, 139
expertise, concept of, 104–17
Eysenck, Hans, 6–7, 12–14, 20,
    22, 33, 35–6, 119, 137

Fairbairn, Ronald, 141
falsifiability principle, 32
family therapy, 67
'fast track' training in psychology, 59
Federation of Practical Psychology
    Clubs, 9
feedback to trainees, 48–9
feminism, 4, 103, 107–8
First World War, 11–12
Firth-Cozens, J., 61
Fisher, R.A., 33
Fleck, J., 114
forensic work of clinical
    psychologists, 82–3
Foster, J., 15
Foucault, Michel, 3–4, 30, 108–9
France, 21
Frankish, P., 96
Freidson, E., 28–9
Fryer, D., 94
fundholding arrangements, 90–1

Gallagher, H., 56
Galton, Francis, 7, 13, 20–1
Gambril, E., 50
'gateway' workers, 55
Gellner, E., 24–5

general practitioners (GPs), 90–1
Germany, 6
Gilbert, P., 132
Goodwin, A., 71
group therapy, 66–7, 69

Hall, J., 5, 61
Hallam, A.M., 9–10
Halliday, T.C., 26, 29–30
Harmon, G., 38
Hayes, D., 88
Head, D., 38
Health Professions Council, 124–5
health psychology, 77–9
Hoffman, R.R., 110, 112
Hollander, Bernard, 9
Holmes, G., 100
'homework', 138
Hoshmand, L.T., 28
House of Commons Select Committee
    on Health, 98
Hull University, 51
humanistic approaches, 37, 44, 104–5
hypothesis testing, 32–3, 36

idealism, philosophical, 110
implicit knowledge, 27
inclusive practice, 76
indeterminacy of knowledge,
    26–31, 40, 50
'index' offences, 83
industrial psychology, 12
in-service training, 60
Institute of Psychiatry, 12–13, 119, 122
intellectual disabilities, 74–6,
    120, 128–9
intern posts, 60
interpersonal psychotherapy, 139
I/T ratio, 26–7

Jacox, A., 43
James, William, 8
Jamous, H., 26–7
Johnson, T., 3
Jones, D., 11, 33–5, 40
Jorm, A.F., 132
*Journal of Community and Applied
    Social Psychology*, 94
Jung, Carl, 141

Kahn, R.L., 48
Kelly, George, 22, 112, 140

Kendell, R.E., 39–40
Kennedy, P., 131
Kinderman, P., 60
Klein, M., 141
Klerman, Gerald, 139
knowledge systems, 25, 111

Larson, M.S., 26, 31, 114
Lawton, R., 85
Leahey, Thomas, 33
learning difficulties, *see* intellectual
    disabilities
Leeds University, 52, 121
legislation on mental health services,
    83, 97–101, 116, 119, 124–8
'level 1', 'level 2' and 'level 3' skills,
    18–19, 105, 107, 111, 113
Levenson, V.L., 98–9
Lewis, Aubrey, 36
lifelong learning, 61
Lindsay, W.R., 92
Linehan, Marsha, 21, 138
litigation work by clinicians, 64
Llewelyn, S., 131
Lloyd George, David, 12
logical positivism, 32–3
London Psycho-Therapeutic Society, 9

Macdonald, K.M., 26–7, 29
McLeod, A., 133
McPherson, F., 90–3
malpractice, 116
managerial role of clinical
    psychologists, 68
managerialism, 17–18, 115, 120, 122
Marks, Isaac, 122
Marx, Karl, 4, 26
Marxism, 3, 103
Marzillier, J., 5
Maslow, Abraham, 133
Maudsley Hospital, 35–7
maximum security hospitals, 83
Medical Research Council, 12
Medlik, L., 90
mental health acts, *see* legislation
Mental Health Alliance, 98
mental hygiene movement, 10–11
Meyer, Adolf, 139
Meyer, Victor, 22, 123
Miller, R., 56, 92–3
Milne, Derek, 86
MIND, 15, 98

monopolization by professions, 26
Moss, D., 87
Mowbray, D., 18–19, 38–9, 105–6
Murphy, G., 21

naïve realism, 135
National Health Service (NHS),
    15–16, 18, 22, 26, 38, 48–54,
    58–61, 64–7, 74, 85–7, 93, 101,
    105, 117–18, 121–7, 131, 134
National Institute for Clinical
    Excellence, 86
national service framework
    for mental health, 55, 72, 96–7, 126
    for older people, 73–4
neurological conditions, 81–2
Niebor, R., 87
'normalisation' movement, 128

older people, services for, 72–4
Olesen, V., 48
Orford, J., 94
Ørner, E.J., 86–7
O'Sullivan, K.R., 38

Padesky, Christine, 21
Pantalon, M.V., 129
Papworth, M.A., 91
Parker, D., 85
Parry, G., 18, 39
Parsons, T., 2, 5
Partridge, K., 87
patient-centred practice, 128
patient liaison groups, 127
patriarchy, 4, 108
Paxton, R., 93
pay structure in clinical psychology, 65
Payne, R.W., 36
Peaker, A., 91
Peloille, B., 26–7
personal construct theory and
    therapy, 22, 107, 137–40
personality disorder, 83, 98, 101,
    126, 138
person-centred therapy, 137–40
physical health care, psychology
    in, 76–9
Pilgrim, D., 38, 62
Polkinghorne, D.E., 28
Polyani, K., 24
Popper, Karl, 32

Positive Psychology movement, 133
postgraduate courses in clinical
    psychology, 52, 58–60
postmodernism, 8, 109, 118, 120
poststructuralism, 3–4, 11, 30–1,
    103, 106–7, 110, 113
post-traumatic stress disorder, 12
Practical Psychologist, 9–10
primary care work, 65, 70–1, 74,
    89–93, 100, 127
private practice, 64, 85–6, 124
proceduralisation of health care,
    85, 88
professional boundaries, 5, 11, 16,
    20, 35, 38–9, 106, 120
professional influence, 3, 29–31
professional judgement, 28, 31
professional socialization, 43, 48–50
professionalization, 24–6, 114, 130
professions
    characteristics of, 1–4, 25–30
    in mental health field, 1–2, 5, 31, 36–7
    sociology of, 103–6, 113
protocol statements, 32
protoprofessionalization, 130
'psy complex', 2, 100, 103–7,
    110–13, 117
psychiatric rehabilitation, 71–2
psychiatry, 16, 20, 30, 35–6, 90, 93,
    99, 118, 122–32
psychoanalysis, 15, 20, 22, 35, 138–41
psychodynamic therapy, 119–25, 140–1
Psychological Therapies Institute,
    Leeds, 121
psychology
    as an academic discipline, 6–8,
        10–11, 17, 121, 134
    experimental, 32–6, 123
    popular, 8–11, 20, 35
    as a science, 31–6
Psychology and Psychotherapy
    Association, 37
psychometrics, 7, 13–14, 20, 35,
    37, 120
psychotherapy, general definition
    of, 136–7

Rachman, Jack, 22
Rachman, Stanley, 123
randomised controlled trials,
    67–8, 122

rational emotive behaviour
    therapy, 138, 141
rationality, 109
Raven, John, 14
Rees, J.R., 12
reflexivity, 110
registration of practitioners, 15–19,
    52, 61, 115, 120, 125
regulation of practitioners, 116, 124
rehabilitation programmes,
    71–2, 76–7, 82
Reisman, John, 21
research by clinical psychologists,
    67–8, 131–2
responsible medical officers,
    98–101, 116
Richards, B., 105
risk assessment, 98
Rivers, W.H.R., 7–8
Rogers, Carl, 111, 133, 139–40
Rose, N., 30–1
Roth, T., 88–9
Rounsaville, B.J., 110
Royal College of Psychiatrists, 98
Ryle, Anthony, 138

Saks, M., 2–3
scientific thought processes,
    innate, 112
scientist-practitioner model, 35–40,
    43–7, 50, 67, 86, 107, 120, 131
scientology, 15
Scotland, 54, 101
Second World War, 12
secure units and services, 83, 128, 134
Seighart Report (1978), 15–16, 125
self-help initiatives, 9–10, 35, 129–31
self-regulation in clinical
    psychology, 15–19
Seligman, M., 133
sexual abuse of patients, 116
Shapiro, D., 121
Shapiro, M., 14, 22, 36, 123
Shaw, George Bernard, 1, 5
shell-shock, 11–12
single-speciality clinicians, 59
skill-mix model of treatment, 92–3
Skinner, B.F., 22
Slade, M., 132
Smail, D., 37, 40
social constructionism, 96

social control, 83, 97–100, 103,
    118, 128
social inclusion, 96–9, 128
solution-focused therapy, 138, 141–2
Spence, M., 95–6
split posts, 64–5
statements of equivalence
    (SoEs), 54–8
Stelling, J., 49
Stevens, S.S., 32
substance misuse, 79–81
Sullivan, H.S., 139
'syncretic' professions, 29–30
systemic theories and therapies, 96

Tavistock Clinic, 12–13, 119, 122
Thatcher, Margaret, 16, 18
therapeutic relationship, 46, 111
Thomson, M., 8–11
tradeability of knowledge, 114–18
training in clinical psychology, 19–20,
    26, 36–8, 42–62, 67, 95,
    110–11, 123–4, 129, 131
    current provision for, 51–5
    funding of, 54
    future prospects for, 55–62
    trainees' perspectives on, 42–51
training of other health professionals
    by clinical psychologists, 67
'trait and function' approach to
    professional work, 2, 5, 104
Treacher, A., 38
Trethowan Report (1977), 15–16, 122

unconditional positive regard, 111
United Kingdom Council for
    Psychotherapy (UKCP), 19, 125
United States, 8, 13–14, 21–2, 36–7,
    72, 85–6, 93, 95, 129, 133
university courses in psychology,
    51–4, 95
user involvement, 127–8
Ussher, J., 108

Vienna school, 32

Walsh, S., 49–50
Wang, Mike, 127
Ward, James, 7–8
Watson, James, 22
Weber, Max, 2, 4, 6, 26

Weissman, Myrna, 139
well-being, concept of, 133
Whittaker, E.W., 48
Wilson, J., 56
Winnicott, Donald, 141
Wolpe, Joseph, 137
women as clinical psychologists,
    5–6, 108

work experience in clinical
    psychology, 42–3, 52–3
Workforce Action Team Report
    (2001), 55

Zadik, T., 86